For God's Sake...
Unity

edited by Maxwell Craig

Wild Goose Publications

CONTENTS

CONTRIBUTORS to *For God's Sake . . . Unity*

MARTIN CONWAY is a lay member of the Church of England, with long experience of working for the world-wide ecumenical movement through the Student Christian Movement, the World Council of Churches, the British Council of Churches and, most recently, as President of the Selly Oak Colleges in Birmingham, from which post he retired in August 1997.

MAXWELL CRAIG is a Church of Scotland minister with parish experience in Edinburgh, Falkirk, Glasgow and Aberdeen, and is a member of the Iona Community; he is presently General Secretary of Action of Churches Together in Scotland (ACTS), based at Scottish Churches House, Dunblane.

JOHN FITZSIMMONS is a Roman Catholic priest whose main interests are biblical studies and liturgy – both in an ecumenical context. He is presently a parish priest in Erskine and Convener of the Unity, Faith and Order Commission of ACTS

KATHY GALLOWAY is a theologian, poet and political activist. She is a member of the Iona Community and editor of its magazine, *Coracle*. She lives in Glasgow, has a Presbyterian background, an Anglican publisher, a Baptist employer and an ecumenical orientation.

GERARD W. HUGHES is a Jesuit priest based in Birmingham, who works ecumenically on spirituality, with a particular interest in individuals and groups who are actively committed to work for justice and peace. His books include *In Search of a Way*, *God of Surprises*, *Walk to Jerusalem*, *God, Where are You?* all published by Darton, Longman & Todd; and *Oh God, Why?* published by the Bible Reading Fellowship.

For God's Sake . . . Unity

MURDOCH MACKENZIE was ordained in South India, worked for three years in Fife as a minister of the Church of Scotland and has been a minister of the United Reformed Church since 1981. Now in his third new town, Murdoch is the second Ecumenical Moderator of Milton Keynes and 'chief pastor' for the sixty-five churches in the city, twenty-four of which are integrated ecumenical congregations.

JEAN MAYLAND is an Anglican priest who taught for many years in schools and colleges and on an ecumenical ordination training course. She has long been involved in the ecumenical movement and currently works for the Council of Churches for Britain and Ireland at the desk for the Community of Women and Men in the Church.

ELIZABETH TEMPLETON is a theologian who has worked in ecumenical circles at local, national and international levels; an occasional writer and broadcaster, she is Development Officer for the Christian Education Movement in Scotland, based in Edinburgh.

INTRODUCTION

'I AM WHO I AM,' says God. He was responding to Moses' question in the Exodus story of the burning bush (Exodus 3.14). Moses was asking the favour of a name to warrant the shaky enterprise which became a triumphant Exodus. Names matter to us. We are glad when our names are remembered with accuracy. They put us into sharp focus: they tell who our parents are and where we come from; they suggest brothers and sisters and our wider identity of kith and kin. The 'I AM' of God is the opposite of our names. It expresses the unbounded majesty of the living God, the creator and sustainer of the universe. There is no limit to God's being. The glory of God breaks the syntax of our language.

The glory of the Church is the worship of God, diverse in its form, one in its purpose. I had the privilege of attending the Second European Ecumenical Assembly in Graz, Austria, in June 1997. Each morning of that week-long event, some 5,000 Orthodox, Roman Catholic, Anglican and Protestant Christians gathered to praise God. Their praise was remarkably diverse – from Taizé choruses, through Wild Goose songs, to Gregorian chants and Orthodox canticles. We ran the gamut of faith-filled music, without trespassing beyond the bounds of our unity in Christ. This was the big assembly in full song. Later each day groups met in tens and twenties all over the city. Their praise was quieter, more reflective, but equally authentic in representing the glory of the Church in worship.

The shame of the Church is its attempt to limit authentic worship to one or possibly a few traditions, regarding the worship of other traditions as less than authentic. This tendency leads to exclusivism. 'I liked the words of that hymn,' says a worshipper, 'but why do we sing it to the wrong tune?' If I come into an unfamiliar church service on a holiday Sunday and I see the number of my favourite hymn on the hymn-board, I feel at home immediately . . . that is, until the organist strikes up what I have the effrontery to call 'the wrong tune'. The 'wrong tune' syndrome is the bugbear of organists and liturgists throughout the Church and it displays the conservative inertia of much Christian worship. A good tune cannot be the wrong tune; it can only be an unfamiliar tune. If such exclusivism were confined to the Church's worship, it would be sad but not serious. What is serious is the determination of many Christians to regard traditions other than their own as handicapped, limited, 'less than the full shilling'. When this determination spills out from Sunday worship into the working world, the dangers multiply. In the West of Scotland, the job interview goes fine until you are asked what school you went to – then the thumbs go down. You want a house in a better part of the city, but the Orange–Green divide is against you. Your children walk a long road to school, because the local school is not for them. We like to think our society, at least east of the Irish Sea, is run on open lines, but ethnic exclusivism is not a Bosnian monopoly.

All down the centuries, Christian men and women have felt the pain of this exclusion. 'The Kirk? It's no' for the likes of us,' say the punters of Govan. And of course Christian ministers rush into their pulpits to say that they have got it wrong, in order to defend the claimed openness of the Church. Rightly so, for that has to be the message of the evangel, the gospel of the Jesus who said: 'Come to me, all of you who are weary and heavy-laden and I will give you rest,' and 'The person who comes to me I will not cast out.' But, in spite of all our welcoming words, that is not how people see the Church.

I visited a handsome church in Italy one holiday morning. Over its west door was written: 'Non patet impiis.' Maybe it sounds less offensive in Latin, but in Scots these words mean, 'It's no' for the likes o' us.'

The Law Society of Scotland has as its motto the slogan 'Nihil humanum alienum puto' – If it's human, it's our business. Edinburgh's Royal Infirmary puts it even more succinctly: 'Open to all.' The Church has a lesson to learn from these secular institutions. That lesson is the theme of this book: an exclusive Church may well have been necessary in the face of persecution, heresies and an antagonistic state, but an inclusive Church is now essential if its message is to be heard clearly.

The chapters that follow are the result of ecumenical team-work: five males and three females; four resident in Scotland and four from England; one from the United Reformed Church, two Anglican, two Roman Catholic and three Presbyterian.

In my experience, there are several kinds of team. Some have fifteen members, some eleven, others eight. There are the eights who strain their flimsy structures with the tide of the Thames from Putney to Mortlake each spring in the University Boat Race. These eights are highly drilled, each oar punching the water at precisely the same moment, arms in unison, lungs bursting as one. There is another quite different kind of eightsome – the eightsome reel, dancing to 'the wind that shakes the barley' – or the wind of God's Holy Spirit. In an eightsome reel, all eight dance to the one tune, but there is scope within the dance for each individual to express his or her own self. The eight contributors to this book are more like an eightsome reel than a rowing eight. Their contributions are distinctive, expressing their widely varying experience, yet all are committed to the cause of Christian unity. But what kind of unity?

There are several answers to this question among ecumenically committed people. Some feel strongly that a single, united or uniting Church is what is required; others prefer 'organic' unity, a single church structure growing, in due course and in God's time, from the grassroots of local congregations; some talk of the 'spiritual' unity we already have in Christ and its flowering; others promote 'visible' unity, claiming that, while diversity must be maintained, whatever unity is achieved must be visible to those beyond our denominations.

As you read these pages, we hope that they will stir your desire for Christian unity; and stimulate the will to put that desire into effect, wherever the opportunity arises within local communities.

There is a great deal of ecumenical talk at national and international level. The sharing of that talk has been vigorously promoted internationally by the World Council of Churches (WCC) and within each nation by the various National Councils of Churches. It is wholly appropriate to celebrate the WCC in 1998, the fiftieth anniversary of its foundation in Amsterdam in 1948. In December 1998 Harare will host the Eighth Assembly of the WCC, where the achievements and disappointments of the past fifty years will form the back-cloth to all the shared prayer, worship and debate. One sobering truth remains: unity achieved at international and national level can sound hollow if it is not also found among local congregations. If it hasn't happened locally, it hasn't happened. That is the continuing challenge to all who are committed to the unity of Christ's Church.

Maxwell Craig

One

PUT YOUR HAND IN MY SIDE
Communities of hope and unity in worship
Kathy Galloway

> *The Lord says, 'I hate your religious festivals; I cannot*
> *stand them! When you bring me burnt offerings and*
> *grain offerings I will not accept them; I will not accept*
> *the animals you have fattened to bring me as offerings.*
> *Stop your noisy songs; I do not want to listen to your*
> *harps. Instead, let justice flow like a stream, and right-*
> *eousness like a river that never goes dry.'*
> *(Amos 5.21–24)*

At the end of the 1970s, I was living in a small ecumenical Christian community in an inner-city housing scheme in Edinburgh.
We were about a dozen adults and six small children, inhabiting a
six-flat tenement in the midst of some fairly serious urban dere-
liction and social deprivation. Every day, we met for worship in
one of our homes. We had moved to live together (most of us
were already living in the area) for a number of reasons: to find
the support and nurture of a Christian community for the task of
living and working in a variety of community-based projects and
churches; as a sign of solidarity with the hard-pressed people of
the area, involved with tenants' groups, housing and school campaigns and the like; and to be a place where the practice of prayer
and witness, Catholic and Protestant together, would go hand in
hand. You can see that our objectives were modest! Well, we were
mostly young, we were very committed, and we were full of enthusiasm. We wanted to change the world – or at least that part of
it we were living in.

Two years on, here we were, sitting in one of our regular, interminable and rather fractious meetings, with our great ideals crumbling around us. We were deeply divided about a number of things – boundary questions about how available we should be for those round about us, how we organized ourselves as a community, and how we participated in the local community. For the past two hours we had been bloodletting, and all of us had been forced to face some things about ourselves we would rather not have faced. Someone began to say what had previously been unthinkable to us – that we had failed, that our community was fated, that perhaps we should think about moving out, moving on.

Suddenly, one of our number who had been silent for a little while broke in, earnestly and calmly, but quite firmly. *'But we love each other,'* he said. The room became quiet. Everyone sat very still. Each of us was recognizing the truth of what he had just said.

Shortly afterwards, the meeting broke up. The community went on. But there was a qualitative difference to our going on. We learned to live, though still painfully and with a lot of struggle, with the community we actually had and not with our agenda for community. We discovered how much we had to learn, and how little to teach, about endurance, resistance and hope from the people round about us. We had wanted to change the world, and discovered how hard it was even to change ourselves.

On 15 September 1984, at 8 o'clock in the morning, I was standing in Iona Abbey ringing the great bell. I tolled it 35 times, once for each year in the life of a man who had died an hour earlier. Brian was a member of the Abbey resident group; he had bone cancer and died leaving a widow and three young children. In the spring of that year, when it became clear that Brian was not going to recover, the resident group had made the decision, at the request of Brian and his family, not to send him away to a hospital or even to a hospice, but to nurse him ourselves in the Abbey and allow him to die in what was then his home, surrounded by his family and friends.

For six months he lived in a flat thirty feet from the refectory where, every week, hundreds of people came and went and ate their meals. As he became sicker, and unable to move about very much, the life of the resident group moved increasingly into Brian's bedroom. In that room, we held our group meetings, ate meals, celebrated communion. Each morning, people would go in to say the words of the morning service with him at the same time that everyone else was worshipping in the Abbey. In the later stages, we bathed him, fed him, turned him, sat and prayed and talked and sang with him. The children played round the bed.

Meanwhile, the busy life of the Abbey went inexorably on. A new heating system was installed and opened. Pilgrimages came from Liverpool and Ireland. The summer programme came and all the day visitors. But as the season went on, more and more the life of the resident group seemed to find its meaning and its momentum in Brian's room. It became like the engine-room powering a great ship. *'In the midst of life we are in death.'*

The effect of this intense and profound experience in our common life was to unite a group of about fifteen disparate people, many of whom had not known each other six months before and all of whom had their own difficulties and problems, in an almost unshakeable bond. We had had to rely on one another, trust one another, do things that sometimes went against the grain, enter into what sometimes seemed like unbearable intimacy, not because the Iona Community had directed us to, or because we were trying to be good Christians, but because it was a matter of necessity.

And here I was, on a Saturday morning of almost unbelievable beauty, aware that in four hours another hundred guests would arrive at the jetty needing to be met, welcomed and fed, ringing the bell for Brian. It was a quite instinctive action on my part. My feet had simply led me directly there. I was, I think, intuitively following the insight of the Orcadian poet George Mackay Brown, who wrote: 'Transfigured by ceremony, the truths we could not otherwise endure come to us.' I wanted to mark the years of Brian's life. I wanted to give meaning to my own grief. I

15

wanted everyone on Iona to know that 'he was here, and now he is not'. And I wanted to communicate what I had learned, that this was not just one man's passing. 'Do not seek to know for whom the bell tolls; it tolls for thee.' (John Donne)

A couple of years ago, I travelled to Aberdeen with a group of people to do a workshop on poverty with a number of churches there. The group all belonged to a movement living in poverty, whose aim is affirming the dignity of poor people, providing mutual support and putting the issue of poverty higher on the public agenda. Coming from Glasgow, this was the first time we had travelled so far afield to do workshops. We had been working hard for weeks on the planning and preparation. We were nervous and excited. We had a very early start for the long train journey, but everyone made it on time – seven adults and four children. It had something of the atmosphere of a day out and everyone was in a positive mood.

We got there safely and found our contacts in Aberdeen. The day went really well. Some very useful connections were made. We were all feeling great; we felt affirmed; we'd achieved something real. The day should have ended perfectly.

Somehow, the journey back turned into the journey from hell. The children were tired, over-excited and not inclined to find the games they had played with on the way up at all interesting. All the drawing paper had been drawn on. And they were getting hungry again, demanding chips, not wanting more sandwiches. None of us had enough money for that. An argument broke out amongst three of the women, the voices and the language getting more heated by the moment. It almost came to blows. The hyperactive child got more hyper and started to rampage through the train. His mother gave up all efforts to control him. The other passengers were beginning to look askance, and to make indirect remarks in loud voices. This nearly precipitated another fight. The day that had started so well seemed to have turned into the most awful shambles.

These three stories illustrate for me three crucial characteristics of what it is to be a community of hope. I think they are characteristic of all communities founded on the resurrection, as they were of the original community of the resurrection constituted by the first followers of Jesus.

In the Stair Community in Edinburgh, that moment when one of us said, *'But we love one another,'* was an absolutely significant moment. You could say it was a fundamental point in the life of our community, because it was the point at *which we were given our name.* Someone had recognized the truth of who we were, and in that instant we had all of us recognized ourselves. We were not the saviours of West Pilton. We had failed miserably in almost everything we had set out to do. We had seen ourselves in a new light, the light of disillusion, and we did not like what we saw. We were despairing. But *'we love one another'.*

Suddenly, the fact that we were wounded, that we had wounded one another, was not as important as the fact that we loved one another. *That* was our bottom line, the rock on which we stood, not our failure. Now we knew our name. We were people who loved one another. That flash of recognition, of being known and named, became a place of gospel, of good news, that we went back to again and again to find ourselves when we got lost. It became our *common story.* We were people who loved each other, who, because we loved each other, could be forgiven and accepted. And each time we went back to that place and knew again who we were, we discovered a new and extended identity. We discovered a new hope.

Mary, stricken and bereft, looking for the lost Jesus in the garden, recognized him when he called her by her name. And not only did she recognize Jesus, but she knew herself again. She was Mary, the loved Mary, the recognized Mary. Peter, guilty, ashamed, knowing only that he had failed the Lord he loved, was named by Jesus – his old name, but with a new invitation to follow, a second chance at love. The disciples on the road to Emmaus did not recognize Jesus until he broke the bread. That was their moment of naming. Because, beyond all judgement, the naming and the knowing were spoken in the voice of love. And when we are named with love, then we hope again. We know that the voice of love is not silenced forever. *Communities of hope recognize their name and tell their story.*

The experience of being part of that resident group on Iona in 1984 was so profound that it marked me for life. It touched on the depths of existence. The bonds formed with the other members were, and remain, very strong. And yet I also know that we were not most a community of hope when we were caring for Brian, or when he died, not even when he was buried in a downpour of rain on Iona and we sang resurrection songs. We were most a community of hope at the very end of that year, when we dissolved ourselves. Some left Iona to go on to other jobs, places, lives; some stayed behind to greet the new resident group members for 1985 and begin all over again. It felt like being broken into little pieces.

Genuine intimacy is a precious and gracious gift. It is rare enough in our depersonalized society for us not to take it for granted. And yet, though it is a gift of community, it is not to be equated *with* community. Intimacy is formed in a 'gestalt', a context with defined boundaries, within which it is safe to be vulnerable, open, and let the masks slip. The intimacy which Jesus enjoyed with his disciples was a natural part of close relations with a group of people over a period of time.

The disciples loved their intimacy with Jesus. They wanted to hold on to it. They grieved for its loss after his death. But they did not yet understand what he had shown them at their last meal together. Intimacy is always exclusive. The boundaries that make it possible, that include us in, always keep others out. This is a perennial problem in churches. We live with a continual tension between those who are on the inside and those who are on the outside, not just of the Church itself, but of the various smaller groupings that co-exist within the Church.

And sometimes we confuse intimacy with being a community of hope. We cannot deny the need and the giftedness of intimacy. It is part of being human. It affirms us, values us. And yet the calling of communities of hope is to accept that affirmation and value – that gift – and take it out into the world. Not to think that we can do without boundaries, but to be ready to break open our *common life* and share it. It is a constant forming and reforming, and we often experience it as a kind of death. But it is the death that brings new life, it is bread broken to be shared. *Communities of hope are always breaking open.*

As I neared the end of that train journey from Aberdeen to Glasgow, l was aware of a knot in my stomach that came from acutely conflicting emotions. I identified at least three of them. The first was the conflict between frailty and power. A few hours before, we had been harmonious, co-operative, each rising to the heights of which we were capable. Now we were quarrelsome, fractious and down in the depths. Lots of reasons for it, of course – tiredness, the release of pressure and, more than these, having been to a mountaintop, however small, and having to go back down to where there was little opportunity for fulfilment, little affirmation, just the daily, relentless grind. It is a transition we know only too well – just when we are feeling particularly elevated, particularly holy, in an instant we turn and snarl most viciously at the children for making a noise. It is a kind of mini, speeded-up fall: from heaven to hell in sixty seconds. A reminder that we always live with sin, the separation from what we are capable of. It is the human condition.

Alongside that was the conflict between familiarity and what I can only call strangeness, a radical dislocation between what had been and what was. It is what sometimes happens to us when we think we know someone very well, and then something happens which make us see them in a totally different light. They become strange, different, absolutely other to us. It is not so much that they are better or worse, it is just that we meet them anew, this time as stranger. This is how the disciples met Jesus after the resurrection, a fearful revelation showing us that what we thought we knew was not, after all, the last word, that there was much more to learn, that God comes to us as much in strangeness as in familiarity. In the otherness, life also lies. Hope comes in strange forms.

And as I sat there, part of me just wished that I could close my eyes, make the strangeness disappear, and find myself anywhere except making this nightmare journey. But part of me wanted to leap up and shout at all the people on the train who were muttering in disapproval, 'Don't you know that, every day, this group of people refuse to accept exclusion and violence and worthlessness as the final word. Don't you know that, every day, they bear witness to the victory of life over death.'

Of course, I didn't do that. But the whole incident crystallized for me the knowledge that that is what communities of hope do – communities of hope *bear witness*, they testify to the conviction that *lostness is not the last word*. That testimony is never perfect. It is good that it often comes in the form of strangeness, because the hope lies not in our perfection or our familiarity, but in our imperfection and our strangeness. The last word is that these too are loved. As the bedraggled group staggered off the train in Glasgow, it was as people who were taking that testimony back into the world, bearing witness not just in their words but in their broken lives. This is the common task to which they had been called.

To be a community of hope, a community of the resurrection – to be the Church – is to be characterized by these three things:

- *a common story:* we are people who have heard our name called by God, and have answered 'yes';
- *a common life:* we are people whose life together is constantly broken open to be shared and enlarged;
- *a common task:* we are people who bear witness to the triumph of life over death.

These, I believe, are the marks of the Church, because they are the marks of Jesus: '*Look at the marks, Thomas – put your hand in my side.*'

In public or corporate worship, these marks should also be visible. We gather to acknowledge our name:

> *I will show love to those who were called 'Unloved',*
> *and to those who were called 'Not-My-People'*
> *I will say, 'You are my people,'*

and they will answer, 'You are our God.'
(Hosea 2.23)

and to tell the story of what that means for our lives. We re-present the breaking open and pouring out of the life of Christ in self-offering. We bear witness in testimony, in thanksgiving, in commitment and prayer for others, to the triumph of life over death. In all of this, we offer up our own lives in all their broken-ness, their suffering and faithlessness, to the grace of God, in the conviction that only in that grace is the redirection and transfor-mation of our brokenness possible. And at the heart of our wor-ship is adoration, the amazed wonder that it is indeed so, the 'being-in-love'. This worship of the community is also known as the liturgy, 'the work of the people'.

An ecumenical formation

I have told these three stories not just because they illustrate what for me are the marks of the Church, but because they are significant markers in my own formation as a Christian. They happened at different times in my life, and with different people. But they have this in common: they happened in the context of engagement with a community of hope, among people who were, in different ways and to differing degrees, marginal to the institutional Church. All of them were profoundly ecumenical situations in which denominational background or adherence was either irrelevant, subsumed into a larger imperative or, in-deed, quite unknown.

That is not to say that denominational formation is unimpor-tant. What shapes us and moves us is never unimportant. The fact that I interpret and understand these three experiences as I do, is, in itself, evidence of my own particular formation.

I come from a housing estate in Edinburgh – a new place, built just after the war to provide slum clearance for Edinburgh's rom-antic but somewhat squalid Old Town tenements. Almost before there were houses, there were churches there: Church of Scotland, Roman Catholic, Scottish Episcopalian. By the grace of God, in those heady days around the Second Vatican Council, the leaders of all three local churches were ecumenically committed – to a new area, a new openness, a new start. So I grew up as a Presbyterian sharing all the festivals of the Christian Year with Catholics and Episcopalians – not just in worship, but also in the conviviality of parties, shared meals and other social activities. St Mark's and St Hilda's were almost as familiar to me as St John's. There were shared study groups and house churches, ecumenical pilgrimages and holidays to places like Iona and Nunraw. There was united action on social issues.

Most importantly for me as a teenager, there was the ecumenical youth group, set up with a focus on justice and peace. Our name was a subversion of the local gang name. We campaigned, fasted, raised money, worked hard at planning and leading worship on justice and peace themes, made a nuisance of ourselves to the clergy, upset the more sedate members of the churches with our all-night and somewhat noisy vigils, gained some measure of awareness of world issues, and, most of all, enjoyed ourselves hugely. In that group I made friendships which have lasted thirty years. It, and the local church context, were my Christian formation. It was, profoundly, an *ecumenical* formation. It was a formation of *active engagement* with the local community and with the wider world. And, as I came to discover, it was a formation in *marginalization*.

In my youthful innocence, I assumed that this is what churches were like, how they got on together, more or less everywhere. After all, we were all *Christians*! Leaving home to go to university in the rather more sectarian atmosphere of the west of Scotland was a shock from which I have never really recovered! But my early experience gave me a perspective which left me, for a while at least, homeless in the Church. When the prevailing church culture in any denomination is one that says, 'Ecumenism – why?', an alternative view that says 'Why not?' has difficulty finding a place to belong.

From that time on, the *oikoumene* has been my starting-point rather than my destination. I trained and was ordained as a minister of the Church of Scotland, and served as assistant minister in an Edinburgh parish. It was here that I came to live in the ecumenical Stair Community, whose story I told earlier. And here, too, the rigours of addressing everything from damp housing to the huge drug problem in the area, and the accompanying stigma experienced by its people, meant getting very rapidly beyond questions of who was Catholic, who Presbyterian, who Episcopalian. In moments of despair, common prayer is not a question of form or theory, but of necessity. In moments of joy, hard-won, every meal together becomes a sacrament of grace.

Since then, twenty years ago, I have only worked ecumenically. I have done work for Catholics, Anglicans, Methodists, Baptists, Society of Friends and a wide range of ecumenical councils and organizations. I have also worked outside the Church, mostly in local community projects and campaigning organizations. Because there are few recognized structures of employment for ecumenical Christians, I have been self-employed for years.

A few years ago, I chose to let my status as a Church of Scotland minister lapse. This means I cannot legally officiate at the sacraments and ordinances of the Church of Scotland. There were a number of reasons for this decision, but perhaps the main one was that I can no longer identify myself with one denomination of the Church. For many people, I will always be seen as a Presbyterian and this decision as simply evidence of a very Presbyterian non-conformism. Others may see it as indulgent, naïve, a desire for freedom without accountability. I prefer to see it as a logical outcome of my ecumenical formation. The ecumenical movement is where I find my membership of the Body.

In all of this, I continue to be a committed and regular worshipper. I worship regularly where I am engaged with a community of hope. At present, this is in a Baptist church. At other times it has been with other denominations. I take the injunction to worship with the local church very seriously. Furthermore, much – perhaps most – of the work I have been invited to undertake in these years has been as a liturgist. I am invited to preach often. I have conducted and co-ordinated worship at a local, national and international level. I have worked in depth on training for worship with local communities, and conducted many worship workshops.

I know that it is conventional wisdom at the moment to bemoan the state of the ecumenical movement, to see the little ship as becalmed or even sinking. I know that there are many who see it as irrelevant to the real church business of their own denominations, the eccentricity of a few. This is not my experience. My experience is of something else: a huge openness, goodwill, curiosity, imagination and creativity in worship bubbling up in a diverse range of contexts and communities. A real yearning among many to pray and worship together in a way which reflects how they act together. Considerable frustration at the casual and patronizing ways in which this yearning is overlooked, reinterpreted or bottle-necked by clergy.

I suspect that those who see the ecumenical ship as sinking may be looking in the wrong places. They are looking at it in and from the denominations. They are looking for it in the institutional Church, rather than out on the open sea.

The place of gospel

It is my faith that the prime mover of the ecumenical movement is the Holy Spirit. I like these words of the Irish Columban missionary priest and ecologist, Sean McDonagh:

> . . . the Holy Spirit is the principle of communion, binding all reality together, the source of all unity. All attraction, all bonding, all intimacy flows from the Spirit . . . from the Spirit comes the great urge to heal what is broken, re-unite what is separated, and re-create the face of the earth.

After thirty years of living and working ecumenically, I am convinced that in every circumstance, where the Holy Spirit leads us, if we choose to follow, is to the place of gospel, of good news. This is the place where the marks are visible, where people hear their names called with love, where people break open their lives to share them, where people bear witness. This is where Jesus finds us, knows us, loves us, heals us, sets us free and calls us to follow him. Furthermore, I am convinced that the place of gospel is rarely inside a church. The place of gospel is the world.

The place of gospel is the world, where women gather at the well, meet the living Christ, are included, respected and called to a ministry of proclamation. So I have encountered a dynamic and committed ecumenical faith, and its expression in worship, among women working together across denominations in a way that leaves many of their male counterparts standing, defending an authority that seems to derive more from the power to control than from the powerlessness of the cross.

The place of gospel is the world, where Dives continues to ignore the beseechings of Lazarus. So I have encountered a dynamic and committed ecumenical faith, and its expression in worship, among poor people and the people who share their lives and their struggle for justice.

The place of gospel is the world, where a prodigal father shows what it means to be generous in human relationships. So I have encountered a dynamic and committed ecumenical faith, and its expression in worship, among counsellors and carers and people with AIDS and community activists who seek to heal what is broken, re-unite what is separated and re-create the face of the earth.

I could go on – about people working in peacemaking, industrial relations, the health service, race relations, among young people. I could go on about local ecumenical projects and communities, the considerable growth in the numbers of people crossing denominations to study everything from the Bible to pastoral care and contemplative spirituality . . . but you know what I am saying. The place of gospel is never abstract or academic. Nor is it theoretical and dogmatic. It is always the place of engagement with the world. It is the place where the Word becomes flesh, where you can see the marks in the side. In all these places of engagement, people pray together, people worship. And what makes it the place of gospel, as it was when Jesus met people, is that there people are seen first and foremost not as

Catholic or Protestant, Jew or Gentile, neighbour or foreigner, but as *human*. None of us, however committed, can ever be fully known or summed up by our labels. We are first of all human. It does not surprise me that this huge amount of ecumenical engagement and worship (I myself have been in touch with at least forty such groups in 1997 alone) seems to be largely invisible in 'official' church circles. This, I venture to suggest, is because those involved are so often marginal to the denominational structures of authority. Women, poor people, young people, people in unsanctioned relationships or unrespectable or risky occupations, and lay people generally, are still overlooked, not consulted and not trusted when it comes to 'official' ecumenism. And since the function of official representatives in ecumenical bodies is all too often to look after denominational interests and maintain denominational 'face', the resulting work and worship is static and sometimes stagnant.

The resident community on Iona, like the Iona Community as a whole, is drawn from many denominations: Quaker and Catholic, Anglican and Methodist, Baptist and Presbyterian. In that diversity is a huge treasury of riches and experience in worship. In the life of the group, of which I was a member for six years, we were always drawing on that store. It is not that these riches are not available, not appreciated and respected in other situations. Of course they are. *But we had something to invest them in.* We had somewhere to use them, to put them to work for the sake of the gospel. We had a shared life and witness. My observation of many 'official' ecumenical acts of worship is that this is where they come unstuck. People meet, lay out their treasures for others to see and admire – and then they pack them away and take them back to their own houses, having done their ecumenical duty.

If we are not engaged together in the world, the place of gospel, how can we be engaged together in worship? Conversely, where people are so engaged, their ecumenical worship, whether it is in a living-room, a hospice, a conference hall or cathedral, outside a nuclear base or inside a prison, has an undeniable reality and authenticity. George MacLeod, the founder of the Iona Community, writing about prayer, said something which I believe also applies to our common prayer:

There are times when our prayer life is refreshing; but analysed, they turn out to be the times when the pressures have been so weighty that you have simply had to go with them to God. But this is precisely the recovery of the knife-edge. The religious moment flows from the practical.

He also said:

When we have wrestled with our state and given it to God, the illuminative becomes our urgent need and not our pious obligation.

This kind of worship is going on all the time. The marks of Jesus are clearly visible in it.

Liturgy, the work of the people, can never be separated from the demanding common task, from the love in action which we believe God requires of us as worship. *The Lord has told us what is good. What he requires of us is this: to do what is just, to show constant love, to live in humble fellowship with our God.* (Micah 6.8) The words of the prophet Micah are no less true today. The humble and faithful desire, not for 'relevance' or doctrinal purity, but to love God, whom we cannot see, by loving our neighbour, whom we can see. The quest to seek out what it means to live in right relationship with friend, neighbour and enemy alike – these find their naming, their struggles, their failures and joys expressed in the liturgy. We do not seek to dialogue and pray with people of other traditions, other faiths even, just so that we can feel good or be 'spiritual'. We do it so that Protestant and Catholic, or Christian and Jew, or Hindu and Muslim, will not beat each other to death on the streets of Glasgow or Jerusalem or Delhi. That is the true measure of the worth we give God in worship, the extent to which we love each other, recognize and respect our differences, do justice, and take the risks of stepping out through the minefields to where we can find a genuine and costly common ground. *'If l am without love, l am a sounding gong or a clanging cymbal ... '*

There are great numbers of people today, many of whom have little or nothing to do with the institutional Church, who are struggling with the question, 'What is your value as a human being?' in a way which is neither simple nor unthinking. Theories of the atonement are no answer in the face of a society that treats such people as practically worthless and often abuses them. To do worship in such a context is to encounter a shocking vulnerability. If we are afraid that this kind of openness will expose us to the expression of our own and other people's weaknesses, prejudices and unacceptable ideas, then we are right. It does. But then we are forced to confront them honestly, to challenge one another, to move to a deeper level of unity in worship than is possible when we simply wrap it all up in fine words and beautiful music.

In the process of naming and symbolizing which is liturgy, all liturgy edits, selects, interprets and conveys meaning. All liturgy is enculturated: it transmits the cosmology, the world-view, of the dominant culture. Of course, we believe that it is also other things – but it is as well we do not forget this often unconscious enculturation. We are so careful now with words, and rightly so, but we live in a visual world. Recently, I took part in an ecumenical anniversary service. The words and music were thoughtful, well chosen, and obviously carefully and sensitively planned. But what people *saw* was a beautiful cathedral, with the congregation in the nave, then, a very long distance away, seated in a long line across the chancel in front of the altar, ten male church leaders dressed in the vestments of their various denominations. It may be that not everyone saw the scene from quite the same perspective as the clergy!

Similarly with our sacraments and symbols. I find I have almost nothing to say about the most anguished focus of our divisions, except that, from certain perspectives, it seems as if the Church simply mirrors the dominant ideology of the world, in which we, the powerful, having bread, decide who will eat and who will go hungry. Truly, this is the sacrament of brokenness.

Every day, my children, and often our friends, and sometimes strangers we hardly know at all, sit down at the table and I feed them. I do not, before I serve them or let them eat, ask them if they have been good, or tell them that they must confess all their wrongdoing before they get anything. I do not question them about their political or religious affiliations or ask them whether they love me, and make that a condition of their eating. I feed them because they are hungry – and because *I* love *them*.

'I hate your religious festivals . . . Stop your noisy songs . . . Instead, let justice roll down like a river, and righteousness like a stream that never runs dry.' When I hear the words *'this is my body'*, I remember the total identification of Jesus with all humankind, with the *oikoumene*, the whole inhabited world. If we get so caught up in the perfection of our remembrance, the beauty of our ceremonies and prayers, our own nourishment, or our own divisions and interests, that we forget that people are still hungry and that we are embodied with them in Christ's body, then we rather miss the point of Jesus, the bread of life. The bread was broken to be shared. That was – and is – the point of the breaking: that the hungry might be fed.

Increasing numbers of people operate out of a relational rather than an institutional understanding of life. They find themselves in relationship – working, campaigning, loving and living – with people across the huge range of faith backgrounds which our secular, democratic, pluralist society embraces (often, it must be said, with greater tolerance, justice and openness than our fearful churches). They in their turn are shaped by this truly ecumenical formation and are less and less ready to settle for the old dispensations, the old dogmatic disputes, which mean remarkably little to those who come new into our churches. So they will increasingly find ways of praying and worshipping, creating meaningful ceremonies, which express their own unbearable truths. They will do this without the institutional churches if they have to, not particularly out of choice but by necessity. And the churches will find themselves standing uselessly on the shore, shouting at the ecumenical boat, ordering it to go in a different direction, telling it that it is not a boat at all. And will the people on board believe them? Or will they be too caught up in the task of sailing the ship together on the open seas, riding the storm, charting their course by the stars, praying for guidance and courage and faith, to even hear them?

Every time I have taken a step outside the denominational, the institutional, the conventional – in worship, in theology, in social and pastoral engagement – there have been plenty of people crying 'wolf', warning me of uncertainty, insecurity, the threat to faith (my own and others'), loss of influence, loneliness, and a whole host of other terrible things. And indeed, such warnings often made me feel very scared. But the reality is very different. Wherever I have gone, *I have never been alone.* I am ashamed even to talk of my insecurities, when the truth is that so many people have lived their whole lives with a much greater degree of uncertainty. They have always been on the open sea and live by faith to a shattering and humbling degree. This is the place where the marks are visible. This is worth everything!

'Look at the marks, Thomas – put your hand in my side.'

Two

UNITY IN PRAYER
Gerard W. Hughes

*Father, may they be one in us, as you are in me and I
am in you, so that the world may believe it was you
who sent me.*
(John 17.21, Jerusalem Bible)

Prayer is as essential to Christian unity as breath is to the body.
Attempts to promote Christian unity which are not grounded in
and inspired by prayer are like trying to bring a skeleton back to
life by rearranging its bones.

Imagine a meeting of representatives from all Christian denominations. They are presented with the following questionnaire which they are to answer in the name of their
denomination:

1. Do you believe in one God?   YES/NO
2. Do you consider striving to be at one with God essential in
   Christian life?   YES/NO
3. Do you believe prayer, the raising of the mind and heart to
   God, to be an essential element in Christian life?   YES/NO

Although one must always be ready for surprises at any gathering of Christians, it is unlikely that any would answer NO to
any of these questions.

When the representatives are feeling more confident, having
filled in this questionnaire with ease, they are presented with a
second:

1. In any given year, what percentage of your Church's time, energy, resources, finances, is spent on working directly with
   other Christian denominations?
2. In working with people of other faiths or of no faith?

3. Does your Church provide regular instruction for its members on private prayer, as distinct from offering public worship?
YES/NO

4. Does your Church encourage its members to have soul-friends with whom they can speak about their prayer experience and its effect on their lives? YES/NO

5. Is the training of such soul-friends or spiritual guides given priority in your Church?
YES/NO

Readers can fill in this questionnaire for themselves! In my experience, I do not think it would be rash to conjecture that the answers to question 1 might range from 0–5%, and to question 2 from 0–2.5%. Questions 3–5 would be answered with NO by at least 90% of the representatives. If any reader can prove these conjectures to be unduly pessimistic, I shall be delighted to hear from them!

The contrast between the answers to the two questionnaires reveals a split in our spirituality which affects all Christian denominations, a split between our words and our actions, between our religious world and the real world, between ourselves and God. So it is not surprising that we are disunited as Christians.

A useful way of recognizing the split in our own spirituality is to try the following imaginative exercise.

There is a ring at your doorbell one evening. On answering, you meet the Risen Lord himself, standing in your doorway. Somehow you recognize, without any shadow of doubt, that it is the Lord. In imagination, what do you do now? Leave him standing there? Tell him to come back on Sunday? Presumably you welcome him in and invite as many of your friends as you can find. In the course of the evening you may find yourself making utterly fatuous statements to the Lord of all creation such as, 'Do make yourself at home.' Jesus gladly accepts your kind invitation.

Now take a two-week leap in your imagination. Jesus is still in your house. How are things at home now? You remember some of Jesus' sayings:

Do you suppose that I am here to bring peace on earth?
No, I tell you, but rather division. For from now on a
household of five will be divided: three against two
and two against three; the father divided against the
son, son against father, mother against daughter,
daughter against mother, mother-in-law against
daughter-in-law, daughter-in-law against mother-in-
law.
(Luke 12.51–53)

You might also remember what the letter to the Hebrews says about Jesus: 'Jesus Christ, yesterday, today, the same forever.' So how have things been over family meals during the last two weeks? What has Jesus said, or done, which has caused tantrums among some members of the family, and who has been leaving the table and slamming the door behind them?

You have invited Jesus to make himself at home, so he is now inviting his friends to your house. Who were his friends in the gospels and what did other people say about them? 'The tax collectors and the sinners, meanwhile, were all seeking his company to hear what he had to say, and the Pharisees and the scribes complained. "This man," they said, "welcomes sinners and eats with them."' (Luke 15.1–2) What kind of people are arriving at your house, what are the neighbours saying about them, and what is happening to local property values?

Having trouble at home and with the neighbours, you might decide to share Jesus' company with your local church, so you arrange for him to give a little talk. You remember the little talk he once gave to the chief priests, the scribes and the Pharisees, assuring them all that the tax-gatherers and the prostitutes would enter the Kingdom of God before they did. He gives substantially the same sermon to the faithful of St Jude's parish church and there is uproar; the parish loses its principal benefactors.

You return home with Jesus. The problem of your life now is what to do with Jesus, for he is causing trouble at home, with the neighbours and with your local church. As he is Lord of all creation, you cannot throw him out of the house, so what are you to

do? Perhaps look around the house with care, find a suitable cupboard, clear it out, clean and decorate it, have good strong locks
put on the door, push Jesus inside, lock the door and place a lamp
and flowers outside. Each time you pass, you can give a profound
and reverential bow. In this way you have Jesus with you always,
but he does not interfere any more in ordinary life.

Each person will imagine this encounter with Jesus differently,
and we could spend the rest of our lives arguing about our different interpretations. This would be a great waste of time, missing
the point of the exercise, which is to illustrate the split in our
spirituality, whatever may be the differences in our detailed
imaginings. This raises a question for all of us: could it be that
much of our discussion and work for Christian unity is a waste of
time, because we are failing to address the split in our spirituality
which afflicts all of us?

Sin is not letting God be God to us and through us. God, in
Jesus, has become one of us. 'God became a human being, so that
human beings might become God,' as St Irenaeus wrote in the
second century. Putting Jesus in the cupboard is a metaphor for
our refusal to let God be the God who dwells amongst us: we
prefer to keep God out of the way – reverently, of course – so
that we can get on with our own affairs, including our religious
affairs, without interference!

The Church has been described as the sacrament of God, a
sign – and an effective sign – of God's dwelling within us and
amongst us. The Church has always understood God's words to
Israel as also applying to all Christians: 'Be holy, as I the Lord
your God am holy.' This is the essence of our lives as Christians,
to mirror and reflect in our lives the holiness of God. All the
rules, regulations, teachings, forms of worship of our churches
are only justified in so far as they enable us, both individually and
corporately, to be living witnesses of the holiness of God.

The difficulty we experience in accepting this call to holiness,
even the revulsion we may feel at this description of Christian
life, reflects the split in our spirituality. What comes to your
mind when you hear the word 'holiness', what images does the

word evoke? I immediately think of statues and stained glass windows portraying saints in states of divine rapture, clutching lilies, a crucifix or a bible, their eyes cast heavenwards. The saints' lives I read as a child left me with the impression that holiness meant spending hours each day in prayer, eating very little, practising constant self-denial and inflicting lots of physical pain on the body. Holiness seemed to be directly proportionate to physical austerity. When being prepared for my first Holy Communion at the age of six, I remember being told that my mind must be on receiving our Lord in Holy Communion, not on the communion breakfast which would follow. I struggled to obey orders, but my mind kept straying back to the thought of the communion breakfast, so I began to think of God as the anti-breakfast God. Subsequent teaching confirmed this impression: God was not only anti-breakfast, but seemed to be anti most of the things I enjoyed!

The holiness of God

What does it mean, this holiness of God, which our lives are to mirror and reflect?

The holiness of God connotes two aspects of God, God as transcendent and God as immanent.

Transcendent means that God is always beyond the limits of our human thinking and imagining, always greater. '"My thoughts are not your thoughts, my ways are not your ways"; it is Yahweh who speaks' (Isaiah 55. 7). Because God is transcendent, always mystery to our human minds, God can therefore never be defined or adequately described, but is always greater than our human categories. God is a beckoning word, calling us out beyond our human conditioning, our limited vision, for we are called to share in the very life of God. 'For his power working in us can do infinitely more than we can think or imagine' (Ephesians 3.21). This call to share in the very life of God is the source of our human freedom. No power on earth, of State or Church, can be the ultimate controller of our lives. When Jesus was tempted in the desert and offered control of the whole world, he rejected Satan's offer with the words, 'You must worship the Lord your God, and serve him alone.'

How are we, earth-bound creatures, to bear witness to this aspect of God's holiness? Pascal wrote, 'I am astonished at the audacity with which people speak about God.' One way of bearing witness to the holiness of God is to acknowledge the inadequacy of all our statements about God.

Canon Max Warren, a former general secretary of the Church Missionary Society, wrote:

> *Our first task in approaching another people, another culture, another religion, is to take off our shoes, for the place we are approaching is holy. Else we may find ourselves treading on men's dreams. More serious still, we may forget that God was here before our arrival.*

Because God is transcendent, always greater than anything we can think or imagine, we must never look on our faith as a package of truths which require no further investigation. 'Faith,' as St Anselm wrote, 'seeks understanding,' and there is no end to its exploration. True fundamentalism means letting God be the foundation of our minds and hearts, and God is mystery. Therefore the true fundamentalist will always be searching, always growing in understanding, will always welcome questioning, will be a careful and respectful listener to Christians of other denominations, to people of other religions and of no religion. 'Fundamentalism', as the word is used today, means the opposite of all this. 'The fundamentalist' now connotes someone who enjoys absolute certainty about their version of Christian faith, who sees no need to explore our beliefs, because such exploration is a sign of weakness, and who is convinced that all their opponents are wrong and lacking in faith. The fundamentalist, in today's sense of that word, fails to bear witness to the holiness of God!

We also bear witness to God's holiness, God's otherness, by our refusal to let any person, group or created thing become the focal point of our entire being. Worshipping God and adoring

God alone means that we are free, enslaved to no person, group or thing, not bound by love of riches, health, honour, status, reputation. Being free in this way, we will not want to control or dominate others, but will rejoice in their freedom.

It is relatively easy to write of the transcendence of God and of how we are to bear witness to it in our lives; it is putting it into practice which is difficult. Prayer is about being still before the mystery of God in whom we live and move and have our being. Years ago, a Dominican friend, Fr Columba Ryan, said to me, 'God is like a tangent.' And I keep remembering the phrase. All our human experience is contained, as it were, within a circumference. A tangent is a straight line which touches the rim of the circumference. Tangents can touch any point of the circumference, but they always lead beyond it. Our word 'ecstasy' comes from a Greek word which means 'standing outside of'. Ecstasy is a state in which we are taken, momentarily, out of the circumference of our normal experience. It is a state which can be induced by drugs with disastrous long-term effects on the user. It is also a state of which the mystics write, a glimpse beyond the circumference of our normal perception. In prayer we focus our attention on God, present in all our experience. Through this focusing, the reality of God slowly dawns on our consciousness and begins to influence our perception of things. When our perception changes, then our actions and reactions also begin to change. This does not normally happen in any sudden and dramatic way, but is a slow and almost imperceptible process, like the growth of a mustard seed. Unless there is this focusing on God in prayer, we can easily remain unaware of God's presence. God is like a silent guest at a party, easily ignored, but if we give the silent one attention, he or she may turn out to be the most interesting person there.

God is transcendent, but God is also immanent, present in all things. God is not an object of our perception, for in God all creation has its being. 'God,' in St Augustine's words, 'is closer to me than I am to myself.' As transcendent, God is the Other, and that is one meaning of holiness. But God, who is immanent, is also holy. What form does holiness take in God who is in all things? And how are we to bear witness to this holiness of God in our lives?

The book of Wisdom, a late book of the Old Testament and the only biblical book to be written not in Hebrew but in Greek, because it was written to explain the nature of Israel's God to the pagans, speaks of God's immanence and transcendence:

> *In your sight the whole world is like a grain of sand that tips the scales, like a drop of morning dew falling on the ground. Yes, you love all that exists, you hold nothing of what you have made in abhorrence, for had you hated anything, you would not have formed it. And how, had you not willed it, could a thing persist, how be conserved if not called forth by you? You spare all things because all things are yours, Lord, lover of life, you whose imperishable spirit is in all.*
> *(Wisdom 11.21–26)*

God's transcendence is expressed in this passage in 'In your sight the whole world is like a grain of sand,' and God's immanence in 'You love all that exists, you hold nothing of what you have made in abhorrence . . . You spare all things because all things are yours, Lord, lover of life, you, whose imperishable spirit is in all.' The holiness of God means both the otherness of God and also the compassion of God for all creation.

If we are to live God's invitation, 'Be holy, as I the Lord your God am holy,' then our lives must bear witness both to God's transcendence and to God's immanence. We bear witness to God's transcendence by our openness to God and to other people, never assuming that we have all the answers, always being ready to listen and learn from others, whatever their Christian denomination, religion, or lack of it, because we believe that God's thoughts are not our thoughts, and God's ways are not our ways. Our faith will impel us to explore, to question, so that we may understand. We also bear witness to God's transcendence by the freedom of our lives, not allowing ourselves to be totally dominated by any created person or thing, not even if the emperor should call himself divine, as the Roman emperors did!

But God's holiness is also to be expressed in our compassion for all creation, reflecting God's immanent presence in all peoples and in all things. This understanding of the meaning of holiness is very different from the notion of holiness with which many of us are familiar: men and women who spend their lives in lengthy prayers and penances, and whose holiness separates them from this world and its concerns.

This understanding of holiness is central to the message of the Old Testament prophets and the teaching of Jesus. The teaching of the prophets is the theme which pervades all the books of the Old Testament, just as the life and teaching of Jesus pervades the New Testament.

The earliest recorded prophet is Amos, who lived in the eighth century before Christ, at a time when Israel was already divided into a northern kingdom, Israel, and a southern kingdom called Judah. The North was affluent and advanced, the South was poor and backward. Amos, a poor shepherd from the South, was called by God to preach to the affluent North. God filled Amos with zeal, but left him short on tact. Amos addresses the fashionable ladies of Samaria:

> *Listen to this word, you cows of Bashan,*
> *living in the mountains of Samaria,*
> *oppressing the needy, crushing the poor,*
> *saying to your husbands, 'Bring us something*
> *to drink!'*
> *The Lord Yahweh swears this by his holiness:*
> *the days are coming to you now*
> *when you will be dragged out with hooks,*
> *the very last of you with prongs.*
> *Out you will go, each by the nearest breach in*
> *the wall,*
> *to be driven all the way to Hermon.*
> *It is Yahweh who speaks.*
> *(Amos 4.1–3)*

The wrath of Yahweh is directed against them because they are 'oppressing the needy, crushing the poor', whom Yahweh loves. Samaria is sinning against God's covenant by failing to bear witness to God's compassion towards the poor and the oppressed. Through the covenant God has entered into a marriage with Israel: 'I shall be your God, and you shall be my people.' Being true to the covenant demands that Israel should reflect this compassion of God in all her dealings, not only with other Israelites, but also with the stranger. This is the constant message of the Old Testament prophets and it is the key to all those frightening and threatening passages which, taken out of context, as they so often are, present God as a thoroughly bad-tempered, vengeful God. The wrath of God is the obverse of God's compassion for all creation, including the oppressors. That is why the wrathful passages are always followed by comforting words.

Jesus is the image of the God we cannot see. The Pharisees and scribes object to the company Jesus keeps. 'This man,' they said, 'welcomes sinners and eats with them' (Luke 15.1–3). In reply Jesus tells three parables: that of the lost drachma, that of the lost sheep, and the parable of the lost son (the prodigal) and the dutiful son. All three parables emphasize the compassion of God for those who are lost. In the parable of the wedding feast, a picture of God's kingdom, God is presented as a father whose one desire is that as many guests as possible should come to the wedding feast of his son. When some of those invited decline the invitation, the father instructs his servants to 'Go to the open roads and the hedgerows and force people to come in to make sure my house is full' (Luke 14.23). In St Matthew's version of the wedding feast parable, the servants return to report to the king that they have brought everyone in, wicked and good alike. In the gospel miracle accounts, the phrase 'He took pity on them' keeps recurring. In Jesus' description of the final judgement, human beings are judged, not on their religious affiliation or their religious observance, but on their practical compassion. 'I was hungry and you gave me to eat, thirsty and you gave me drink, naked and you clothed me . . .' When the chosen ask, 'But when did we see you hungry and feed you, or thirsty and give you drink?', the

king answers, 'I tell you solemnly, in so far as you did this to one
of the least of these, you did it to me' (Matthew 25.35ff.).

The compassion of God

The God whom Christians worship is a God of compassion. Formal worship which is not a true expression of our desire to be at
one with the God of compassion is abhorrent to God, as the
prophets make clear. Through the prophet Amos, God tells the
people of Samaria what he thinks of their formal liturgies:

I hate and despise your feasts,
I take no pleasure in your solemn festivals.
When you offer me holocausts I reject your oblations,
and refuse to look at your sacrifices of fattened cattle.
Let me have no more of the din of your chanting,
no more of your strumming on harps.
But let justice flow like water
and integrity like an unfailing stream.
(Amos 5.21ff.)

And God speaks the same message through the prophet
Isaiah:

Bring me your worthless offerings no more,
the smoke of them fills me with disgust.
New Moons, sabbaths, assemblies –
I cannot endure festival and solemnity.
Your New Moons and your pilgrimages
I hate with all my soul. They lie heavy on me,
I am tired of bearing them. When you stretch out
your hands
I turn my eyes away.
You may multiply your prayers, I shall not listen.
Your hands are covered with blood,
wash, make yourselves clean.
Take your wrongdoing out of my sight.
Cease to do evil.
Learn to do good,

41

search for justice,
help the oppressed,
be just to the orphan,
plead for the widow.
(Isaiah 1.11ff.)

What is said of formal worship by the prophets can also be applied to our church structures, organization and activity: they can only be pleasing to God in so far as they are effective means for witnessing to the compassion of God for all creation.

The unity of Christians will develop in proportion to the witness each denomination gives to the compassion of God, not only for other Christians but for all human beings and for all creation. Luther described the Church as *'Ecclesia in se incurvata'*, a Church turned in on itself. As long as parishes, churches, Christian groupings are primarily intent on their own survival, directed to maintenance rather than mission, there can never be Christian unity, no matter how well organized individual churches may be, how committed and loyal individuals are to their particular church or parish, how many theologians ponder the question of unity, or how many ecumenical meetings take place.

Christian unity can only be recovered in so far as Christians are God-centred. The most effective work any of us can do for Christian unity is to let God be God to us and through us. To be Church-centred is not necessarily to be God-centred. Idolatry, which means allowing some created thing to take the place of God in our lives, can take many forms. Religious people are always in danger of becoming idolaters, allowing the particular teachings or forms of worship of their church to take the place of God. Such forms of idolatry are both subtle and destructive of our humanity, and history is strewn with examples of them. The temptation is subtle because the idolatry masquerades under the appearance of dedication to God, fidelity to God, loyalty to Christ, so that in God's name we can feel justified in ignoring, condemning, oppressing, exploiting, killing others. If this seems exaggerated, then reflect on the conflicts of this century where the antagonists fought in the name of God, and on the fact that today we are still divided into many opposing churches and sects. These churches and sects can only remain in this divided state because they are convinced that they are right and that those who oppose them are wrong. What divides us cannot be of God, for God is one. Therefore, in our separate denominations we must be clinging on to something which is not of God, but which we are claiming is of God. In all our denominations we are guilty of this and until we acknowledge our guilt there can be no reconciliation. Discovering how we are to be reconciled will take time, but until we acknowledge our own guilt in the dividedness of Christians, the reconciliation process cannot begin.

This chapter, so far, has been mostly scriptural and theological. The God of Abraham, Isaac and Jacob, the father of our Lord Jesus Christ, is the God now holding us in being. The point of reading the Scriptures is to help us recognize this same God at work in us now. Theology is the attempt to formulate in words our experience of God now. When theology loses touch with our experience, it becomes a sterile discipline. In the rest of this chapter I shall try to illustrate, through lived experience, the content of the first part.

I first became interested in ecumenism in the 1950s, but my understanding of it at that time was that all Christian Churches should be united with the Roman Catholic Church! When I went to Germany in 1956 to study theology, I learned of a movement called 'Una Sancta', founded by a Catholic priest, Franz Josef Metzger, who was later executed by the Nazis. The Una Sancta movement was based on the truth that the Holy Spirit is the source of the Church's unity. The more open Christians are to the Holy Spirit, the Bible and their own tradition, the more unity will develop among the churches in ways we cannot yet foresee. All we can be sure of is that whatever form unity may take, it will be consistent with the Church's tradition, of which Scripture is a part. This understanding of Christian unity was a great relief: one no longer had to try and persuade everyone to become a Roman Catholic!

The Second Vatican Council with its decree on the nature of the Church and Ecumenism which recognized the action of the Holy Spirit in other churches, stimulated ecumenism worldwide. There were frequent meetings between the churches and their theologians, annual weeks of prayer for church unity, and co-operation on a scale hitherto undreamed of. I took part in many ecumenical meetings and services, and although I welcomed these moves towards co-operation, I was always conscious of our divisions and of a measure of strain in our ecumenical encounters. As there was always plenty to do within my own denomination, the temptation was to give ecumenical activity a low priority.

Sometimes the nature of the dividedness was clear (for example in doctrinal questions), but discussion on these differences, although it might clarify some points, did not remove the divisions, which seemed to be deeper than our conscious reasoning could grasp. It was only much later, when working on spirituality with Christians of different denominations, that I began to understand why discussion of our doctrinal differences and formal worship together during the week of prayer for Christian unity cannot, of themselves, bring about church unity.

When I worked for eight years as a University chaplain at Glasgow University in the late 1960s and early 1970s, I met many people of different denominations, different faiths and no faith. Most of these people were not much concerned with doctrinal differences between the churches, but they did believe in the value and importance of human life, and many of them were very committed to some form of peace and justice work, a commitment which I found less obvious in many of the more dedicated church members. In fact, I found that the more committed people were to social justice issues, the more critical they were of the Church as they experienced it. I knew then that I wanted to work on spirituality.

Towards a true spirituality

In the late 1970s and early 1980s I worked at a Jesuit spirituality centre at St Beuno's in North Wales. Ignatius of Loyola, a Basque nobleman born in 1493, who had a conversion experience while convalescing after being wounded in battle, wrote a little book called *The Spiritual Exercises*. When he wrote the book he was a layman, theologically illiterate and with no formal training in spirituality. The book is a series of scripture-based, Christ-centred meditations and contemplations. The Inquisition was not happy with this uninstructed layman giving his Spiritual Exercises, so they clapped him in prison, examined the book and could find nothing heretical in it, but forbade him to give these exercises to others until he had become theologically qualified. Ignatius ended up at Paris University, took his degree and collected round him a group of friends who eventually became the first members of the Jesuit religious order. One of the early Jesuits, Jerome Nadal on being asked for whom the Spiritual Exercises were suitable, replied, 'For Catholics, for Protestants and for pagans.' This remark fascinated me and we tried at St Beuno's to ensure that anyone was welcome, irrespective of their denomination or lack of it, and a great variety of people, including some card-carrying Communists, began to come to experience the Spiritual Exercises.

While working at St Beuno's I began to notice that if those who came to do the Spiritual Exercises were actively committed to some form of justice, peace or reconciliation work, they tended to develop spiritually more quickly and deeply than those who were not so committed, yet they often felt alienated from their own church. I also knew that the majority of people committed to peace and justice work did not have the time, the money or the inclination to come to a retreat house, so I asked my Jesuit superiors if I could work ecumenically with people actively committed to justice and peace, going to them rather than expecting them to come to a spirituality centre.

After a year of working with such groups, I began to reflect on

45

a catechism answer which I had learned as a child. The question was, 'What are the marks of the one true Church?' The answer was, 'The Church is one, holy, catholic and apostolic.' This was followed by further questions and answers, showing that these marks were to be found in the Roman Catholic Church and in no other! The peace and justice groups with which I worked included people from a variety of Christian denominations and some who belonged to none, but I began to notice these four characteristics among them.

The Church is one. There was a sense of unity among these very disparate people, a unity in their longing for peace and the promotion of justice. In the retreats that I organized for them, these very different people prayed in silence, individually and together, and we experienced a real unity in Christ, in spite of our differences. When people of different Christian denominations pray together in silence, it is as though they meet at a level deeper than their church and cultural differences, and discover a unity of mind and heart in Christ.

The Church is holy. Most of the people with whom I worked did not think of themselves as holy, or have any desire to be holy, as they understood holiness. For most of them, being holy meant being withdrawn from the world and its concerns, praying for hours each day and practising great austerity. If they had understood holiness as bearing witness to the compassion of God for all creation, they might have recognized their own call to holiness. Because they felt for the poor, the powerless and the victims of injustice, because they were appalled at the prospect of mass destruction by nuclear war in the name of national security, they sacrificed their time, money, prospects. The Greenham women, for example, lived in the open, some of them for years, in a most austere way which would have tried even the early Christian Fathers of the desert, who did not have to endure a British climate. Others endured imprisonment for peace protests, sometimes in horrific conditions.

The Church is catholic. In its literal meaning, catholic means universal, which does not only mean that the Church is to be open to all peoples of all races, cultures, classes. It also has to embrace every aspect of life, all our relationships with each other and with ourselves. The people engaged in peace and justice work had this catholic characteristic, for they felt a kinship with their oppressed brothers and sisters wherever they were – behind the Iron Curtain, among the poor of the Third World, or in our own country. They were also conscious of the damage we do to the animals, plants, rivers and oceans by our consumerist culture, and many of them deliberately chose to live a very simple lifestyle.

The Church is apostolic. Literally, the word 'apostolic' means 'sent'. Jesus' friends were sent to preach the gospel to the whole world, hence the name 'apostles'. Many people working for justice and peace have told me that they were tempted to abandon their task, but found they could not. Their commitment to peace and justice was not something they had chosen, but something which possessed them, disturbed them, and could not be ignored. They understood, from personal experience, the meaning of Jesus' words to his disciples, 'You did not choose me, but I chose you.' In this sense they are apostolic, sent, and like the apostles, seized by Christ.

When I first began working with justice and peace groups, I described what I was doing as 'justice and peace spirituality'. Later, I realized that there is no such thing as justice and peace spirituality. There is one God, one Spirit, a God of justice, of peace, of compassion. Any spirituality which ignores issues of justice and peace cannot be of God.

The split nature of our spirituality is reflected not only in the divided nature of our churches in their relationship to one another, but also in the divisions within each denomination. The division between members of one denomination can be sharper and more bitter than the division between denominations. For example, within every denomination today there is a split between those who limit spirituality to activities formally labelled 'religious': Sunday services, prayer, whether public or private, bible reading, spiritual reading, church activities, etc., and those who are activists in social and political life. The 'spiritual' often complain that the activists are the most disruptive members of their community, pursuing peace and justice in ways which are aggressive, unjust, intolerant and unkind. These objections are often justified and need to be addressed.

Those who become involved in the active promotion of justice and peace are often themselves surprised at the strength of negative emotions which overwhelm them when they meet with the deafness, blindness, selfishness and self-righteousness of those who oppose them, sometimes including their own family and friends. The opposition they meet can reduce them to a state of cynicism about religion and human nature, or to depression and despair. This is where spiritual help is so essential, to enable them to recognize that this crisis, although dangerous, is also an invitation to growth in Christ. Learning to look at their own anger or despair, they can begin to see that it may arise out of injustices and hurts in their own lives which they have never resolved and which they now project on to any who oppose them. Or they may see that much of their pain comes from an assumption that they can overcome injustice by their own efforts, without the need of God's help. Their anger is very often because their vision and their plans are not being recognized, because the focus of their attention is their kingdom rather than God's kingdom of truth, justice, love and compassion.

Through prayer we can begin to see more clearly the relationship between the outer and the inner worlds in which we live, and so realize that we cannot work effectively for unity between churches, or between any opposing groups, until we have learned to live in unity with ourselves. Otherwise we shall only project the disunity within us and inject it into the divisions which already exist.

Where there is disunity within any Christian church between 'the spiritual' and 'the activists', both sides are wrong and both sides need each other.

The 'spiritual' people, who consider any active involvement in peace and justice issues to be a contamination of true religion, have not read the Bible and cannot be at one with the God of compassion. They are refusing to be holy as the Lord our God is holy.

The activists, who commit themselves to issues of peace and justice, but ignore prayer, are in danger of acting aggressively and unjustly towards their opponents or sinking into cynicism and despair. The Bolshevik revolution began with the highest ideals and ended in mass persecution, murder and destruction.

St Paul writes:

> *The Spirit comes to help us in our weakness. For when we cannot choose words in order to pray properly, the Spirit himself expresses our plea in a way that could never be put into words, and God, who knows every-thing in our hearts, knows perfectly well what he means, and that the pleas of the saints expressed by the Spirit are according to the mind of God.*
> *(Romans 8.26–27).*

The psalmist says, 'Be still and know that I am God' (Psalm 46). The ultimate purpose in all our prayer is that we should be still so that God, the God of unity and of compassion for all creation, prays in us. Through prayer we shall be drawn into unity and into working together for the promotion of justice, peace and reconciliation.

In conclusion, all Christians pray, 'Thy kingdom come.' Jesus prayed, 'May they all be one. Father, may they be one in us, as you are in me and I am in you, so that the world may believe it was you who sent me' (John 17.20–21). To work for the unity of Christians is not an optional extra for the more extrovert: it is the duty of every Christian. Asked whether they agree with this statement, no representative of a Christian denomination, at the meeting with which the chapter began, is likely to answer, 'Certainly not.' The sincerity of our answer, that to work for the unity of the Church is the duty of every Christian, can be tested by our answers to these two questions:

1. Does your Church provide regular instruction for its members on private prayer, as distinct from offering public worship?

2. Is the training of soul-friends or spiritual guides given a priority in your Church?

Three

UNITY IN BELIEVING

Jean Mayland

In late 1997 and early 1998 there was a furore in the English press about the appointment of a new Bishop of Liverpool in the place of David Sheppard. There were strong claims that the Prime Minister had rejected the first two names offered to him and asked for two more. Letters appeared in the press which demanded the appointment of a 'traditionalist bishop' who would uphold the authority of the Bible and teach morality. Accusations were made that to appoint a 'liberal' bishop would weaken people's faith and divide the Church. Claims were made that the Church of England had been seriously damaged by earlier 'liberal' bishops.

This is a cry frequently heard in the Church of England in the last few years. It is a desire that seems to affect my church more than any other in these islands. I suppose those in the Roman Catholic Church who want a firm, clear line on the faith get it from their bishops. In the Free Churches there is naturally a greater freedom in believing (and no bishops) and so the issue does not arise. In the Church of England, some people do want just a narrow stream of faith, while others of us want a broad river, and so the conflict simmers on to be fanned into flame by such issues as the one with which I began this chapter.

A bishop condemned and loved

One of the bishops whom some considered to have been a typical 'liberal', weakening the faith of the Church and threatening its pattern of believing, was David Jenkins. He was condemned by people in the Church, pilloried by the tabloid press and subjected to snide remarks by the broadsheets. David Jenkins was also attacked in the General Synod of the Church of England, because he rejected the virgin birth while affirming the incarnation and cast doubt on the empty tomb while proclaiming the resurrection. The House of Bishops considered his words and in their report affirmed the fact that incarnation and resurrection are the vital elements of believing, not virgin birth and empty tomb. This did not satisfy the House of Laity of the General Synod, who took the witch hunt further – not satisfied until they had passed a motion condemning the bishop, in spite of the opposition of a small remnant which included myself.

Yet David Jenkins was not doing anything new. At the time when he was consecrated Bishop, my husband was Canon Treasurer of York Minster. We lived in a lovely old house in Minster Court which fifty years before had been occupied by the scholarly Dean Bates while the new Deanery was being built. In 1938 he piloted through Convocation a Measure which said that the faith of the Church of England lay in an acceptance of the incarnation and resurrection and not necessarily of the virgin birth or the empty tomb. He was also involved in the Faith and Order Movement, one of the strands of which was later woven into the World Council of Churches. In addition, he was involved with the Archbishop of York in some of the early contact with the Russian Orthodox Church. We thought of this when we had Archbishop Kyrill of Russia to stay with us in the 1980s. Because of my interest in doctrine, liturgy and the ecumenical movement, in that house I often felt near to the spirit of the man.

In 1993 I left York and went to work in Bishop David's Diocese of Durham as Diocesan Ecumenical Officer (an Anglican post) and county Ecumenical Officer (an Ecumenical post).

The situation in Durham was very different from the one caricatured in the press or denounced in the General Synod. In the diocese people loved their bishop.. They loved him because he was warm and friendly. They loved him because he was there at the pit gates when the last pits were being closed. They also loved him because he gave them permission to ask questions. I got this from all sides – from people in the parish, from women in the ecumenical women's groups, from people outside the Church and from Christians of all denominations including Roman Catholics and the Salvation Army.

One Salvation Army officer, an ex-miner who was a fellow magistrate in Peterlee, told me just how much he had been encouraged by Bishop David to realize that right believing could well include expressing doubt, asking questions and even rejecting some conventional or conservative concepts. It was not that my Salvation Army friend was willing to believe just anything. I remember one morning in court when we were doing a lot of routine things, with frequent adjournments for lawyers to discuss, we repeatedly walked solemnly out of court to the retiring room and there resumed our discussion about homosexuality and the 'authority' of biblical references. Yet the very fact that we could have such a discussion and that he felt free to consider a variety of views on the authority of the Bible was the result of the freedom he felt he had been given by the bishop. It also provided some stimulating listening for the third member of our bench who chipped in from time to time with his own comments!

In the last Lent of his episcopate (March 1994), Bishop David gave four lectures which he repeated in various large centres of the diocese such as Darlington Town Hall, where I attended. The lectures were packed out, with waiting lists for the tickets which were free. The lectures had the general title 'Good God!', and as weekly titles 'God in the Beginning', 'God in the Mess', 'God in the End', 'God on the Way'.

I well remember attending the first one in Darlington Town Hall. David Jenkins just sat on a table for an hour and talked about God. I remember thinking: I have never heard a bishop just talk about God for an hour before. Then he wandered around the huge hall with his roving mike and answered questions, which flowed thick and fast.

In that first lecture he commented cheerfully: 'Another thing that I have discovered over recent years, and which I believe to be clearly reflected both in history and in the Bible, is that even the Church cannot keep a good God down.'[1] Nearer the end of his lecture he summed things up by saying:

> *In our pluralistic and confused society, I believe that*
> *all this points to a renewed and renewing understand-*
> *ing of what it is to be a Christian. We are called – along*
> *with other believers in God, and with would be seekers*
> *after value who know nothing of God, or say they*
> *know nothing about God – to rediscover the point*
> *about God. This point about God is that He is there to*
> *surprise us all; that She is there to care for us all; and*
> *that It is there to show us all that the mystery goes be-*
> *yond the traps and limitations of all languages, all con-*
> *cepts, all formulae, as well as beyond the traps of all the*
> *pessimisms and depressions we get caught into. The*
> *mystery is there to take us forward.*[2]

A pilgrim people

What a wonderful phrase – 'The mystery is there to take us forward.' This is the theme of much of the Old Testament. At the
burning bush Moses was introduced to Yahweh, the God who
'just is'. Moreover he will 'cause to be what will be'. The Hebrews
must not expect to see or touch God or carry him around as a
statue as the Egyptians did, but they would experience his presence as they journeyed back to the Promised Land. They would
know him as they travelled on their journey. So the first five
books of the Bible, the Pentateuch, are the story of a journey.
Throughout the Pentateuch there is movement, journeying –
nothing is ever static, everything goes forward with and through
the God who causes all to be; but this movement allows freedom
of choice and that choice can be wrong.

Even when the choice is wrong, God's love and compassion
can bring good out of evil. At the end of the Pentateuch we are
left at a point of tension or expectation: the goal of the journey
has not been reached and Israel's leader, Moses, the dominant
human figure since the beginning of Israel, is dead. Israel's future
is open-ended and perhaps even in jeopardy; and yet, as we see in

the next book, the book of Joshua, they go on.

Most scholars believe that the books of the Pentateuch were written in their present form during the Exile in Babylon from 597 BC onwards. To the people in exile the Pentateuch explained their condition and also gave hope for the future – a hope dependent on the nature of God and their freedom to choose. In the words of David Clines of Sheffield University, in his book *The Theme of the Pentateuch*: 'the theme of the Pentateuch is entirely concerned with a future bound to a past out of which the present lives.'³ In other words, not only was the Pentateuch describing a movement to the Promised Land, but the whole point of telling the story was to encourage people to learn from the past how to move on to new things – how to keep on journeying.

The trouble today with so many Christians is that they look to the past in order to stay where they are or move backwards. People want to hold on to past traditions, to cling to some claimed 'simple faith', to grasp what they describe as the traditional sound belief, the biblical truth, apparently unable to see that at the heart of the Bible is the pressure to be pilgrim people, to move on. Admittedly, by the time of Jesus many of the Jews had begun to look back – to cling to their traditions, to follow the law with scrupulousness. Jesus did not follow that line. Jesus claimed that he had come to make all things new. He was never afraid to challenge the *status quo* or the tradition and to urge that no one could put new wine into old wineskins.

What kind of unity in the New Testament?

Yet today people look back to the New Testament and claim that there one can find the truth – the only kind of right believing. When we actually look at the New Testament it is not nearly as easy as that. To begin with, we have four accounts of the ministry of Jesus culminating in each case with his death and resurrection. Even a cursory reading of these four documents reveals that, while there are many similarities, there are also surprising differences and a number of places where it is difficult or even impossible to reconcile the various accounts. Each one was written from a particular standpoint to meet the needs of a particular situation; and information about Jesus is interpreted in different ways to help convince the readers the evangelist had in mind.

The scene becomes even more complicated when we read the stories in the Acts of the Apostles or try to compare the various letters of Paul, Peter or John.

In his book *Unity and Diversity in the New Testament*, James Dunn raises the basic question:

> *Was there ever a single orthodoxy within primitive Christianity, within the New Testament?' Even more basic, can we properly use the concepts 'orthodoxy' and 'heresy'? Is it meaningful to speak of 'orthodoxy' within the context of first-century Christianity?[4]*

He also puts the same question more simply and in less emotive terms:

> *Our basic question thus becomes:* Was there a unifying strand in earliest Christianity which identifies it as Christianity? *If so, how well defined was it? Was it a broad or a narrow strand?[5]*

His conclusion is that in the New Testament there is a considerable diversity, although it is possible to 'speak of a unifying core for the post-Easter kerygma at any rate'.[6]

The 'kerygma' is the basic teaching, preaching or message. If we look at the gospels, the basic 'kerygma' of Jesus was that 'the kingdom of God is at hand' and so the people must 'repent and believe in the gospel'. If people did this, then they could participate in the end-time reign of God. In this, Jesus saw himself as the instrument of the end-time rule, but not as an object of faith.

In the Acts of the Apostles and the epistles of Paul, the core of the kerygma had a rather different outline. It was as follows: Jesus was born of the line of David and his coming fulfilled the prophecies. His miracles showed that he had the power of God, but in spite of this he was crucified, died, was buried and rose again. He is exalted to the right hand of God and will come in judgement.

Those who put their faith in him will enjoy eternal life.

Professor Dunn thinks that there is a wide diversity in the expressions of this kerygma and some aspects of this diversity seem incompatible. He also recognizes that it is difficult to speak of a unity between the post-Easter kerygma and the kerygma of Jesus. In his view a basic question is 'Can we discern sufficient continuity between Jesus the proclaimer and Jesus the proclaimed to enable us to affirm that the kerygma of Jesus and the kerygma of the first Christians are ultimately one and the same.'[7] In the end, he concludes that

> *there is a Unity between the historical Jesus and the kerygmatic Christ. That is to say, the identity between the man Jesus and the proclaimed Christ unites not only the diverse kerygmata in one, but unites also the pre-Easter proclamation of Jesus with the post-Easter kerygma of the first Christians.*[8]

But he also says, 'Diversity is much more obviously a feature of the beginnings of Christianity than the unity . . . *Diversity is as integral to first-century Christianity as unity. In short there is no single closely defined Christianity or christology in the NT.*'[9] In other words, there is not just a narrow stream of faith in Jesus in the New Testament, but a great wide river with many currents. The 'simple, narrow faith' in which many people inside the Church seem to want to believe today has no basis in the New Testament. There is a basis for faith there – but it is wide and encompasses a great many different, sometimes even contradictory, views.

The kerygma and the creeds

In the Acts of the Apostles we are told that those who expressed their faith in Christ were baptized. As time went on a system of training developed for baptism and initiation into the Church. The local bishop gave lectures leading to the rite of initiation, which took place on Holy Saturday night, so that the baptized

would be baptized into the death of Christ and then rise to receive his life into their own at the Eucharist very early on Easter
day. These lectures were commentaries on the basic kerygma
which was taught to the candidates and came, in time, to be sum-
marized in a kind of credal form. Originally, three long questions
about their faith were put to candidates; they were required to
assent to them and then after each response they were dipped
under the water. In time the candidates had to learn this creed by
heart and recite it back before being baptized. Even then the
creed fell naturally into three parts.

The creeds and the bishops' lectures varied from place to place
and obviously developed as a result of local situations or particular questions which arose in certain localities. In her book *The
Making of the Creeds*, Frances Young comments: 'Creeds did not
originate, then, as "tests of orthodoxy", but as summaries of
faith taught to new Christians by their local bishop, summaries
that were traditional to each local church and which in detail varied from place to place.'[10]

On the issue of variations, Professor Young says:

> *There is a sense in which the creeds are not themselves
> a system of doctrine. The variations confirm this obser-
> vation: the discrete points are perhaps less important
> than the bearing they have on the whole. It's as though
> the essential content is indeed a story, and as we all
> know, there are various ways of telling the same story
> depending on the selection of the material, if not the
> artistry of the narrator. These features are important
> pointers to the fundamental nature of the creeds: they
> are summaries of the gospel, digests of the scriptures.*[11]

Moreover these creeds were originally used in worship. They
were expressions of faith or the songs of the faithful – hymns,
not formulae.

In time, however, under pressure from the emperor, the nature
of the creeds began to change. Gradually they came to be regarded as tests of orthodoxy. Bishops began to defend their particular way of teaching and expressing that teaching in a credal

statement. Controversies began to arise about exact nuances of words or the reliability of statements. The growth of what became regarded as heretical teaching pushed bishops and scholars into trying to define and regularize the faith. Councils were called to discuss approaches and argue about the use of words. The final development in this movement came when the emperors began to use their power and influence to enforce the acceptance of a particular viewpoint. Right believing came to depend on the desires of the ruler. Again, as Frances Young puts it, 'imperial and political pressures induced the Ecumenical Councils to use creeds to define acceptable orthodox belief in a search for unity which would inevitably and paradoxically exacerbate division'.[12]

Those who want the churches today to use the creeds to test orthodoxy or define heresy should remember the imperial influence and not just accept them as pure and primitive gospel.

This is not to dismiss the value of the creeds as expressions of truth. To quote Frances Young once more:

> *For the idea of 'orthodoxy' cannot but breed intolerance. But the results are not merely negative: concern about truth, about the way things really are, was also the fruit of this distinctive feature – and surely was a driving force indispensable to human development. Perhaps it is no accident that science was conceived in the womb of a Christian civilization.*[13]

Divisions in the Church

As time went on, of course, the situation hardened still further. Not only were all Christians required to believe the same things, but they were also required to do the same things. Uniformity of practice as well as of belief became compulsory. For centuries Christianity had held together in a unity which contained an amazing amount of diversity – diversity of teaching and practice, kerygma, credal formulation and liturgy. As insistence upon uniformity in belief and practice increased, it consequently became more and more difficult to hold the diversity within the unity. In

59

1054 came the first great split between East and West, ostensibly over the 'filioque' clause in the creed (i.e. the phrase 'and the son' connected with the statement in the Western creed that the Holy Spirit came from the Father and the Son), although it was in fact also the culmination of many other things such as separate developments in liturgy and other areas of theology. This breach was deepened by the Western crusades in the East.

Then came the enormous splintering of the Reformation and the development of the Protestant churches – Lutheran, Calvinist, Reformed, and the Church of England which claimed to be both Catholic and Protestant.

Slowly Christians came to realize the scandals of their divisions and began to seek again a unity which was clearly visible to the outsiders whom they had a duty to bring into faith.

The World Council of Churches and unity in believing

Eventually, the World Council of Churches (WCC) was constituted at its first Assembly in Amsterdam in August 1948. Two 'ecumenical streams', those of the Faith and Order and Life and Work movements, merged at this first Assembly. A third stream, the missionary movement, was integrated at the third Assembly in 1961.

According to its constitution, the primary purpose and function of the World Council of Churches is to 'call the churches to the goal of visible unity in one faith and in one eucharistic fellowship'.

The exact nature of the visible unity which we seek continues to be the subject of much discussion. Is it conciliar unity, or structural unity, or reconciled diversity, or what? The one thing that we seem to be agreed about is that unity does not equal uniformity.

Some of the essential conditions and elements of visible unity have been identified by the Faith and Order Commission of the WCC as follows:

• the common confession of the apostolic faith
• the mutual recognition of baptism, eucharist and ministry

- common structures for witness and service, as well as for decision making.

The Faith and Order Commission worked on questions of baptism, eucharist and ministry for many years. They produced the Lima Report on these issues, which was widely discussed by the churches; their responses fill many volumes. This process in its turn had an effect on many bilateral or multilateral dialogues and was a contributing factor to the progress made in relations between some churches. For example, discussion between the Church of England and the Churches of the Evangelische Kirche in Deutschland (EKD) led to the Meissen Agreement and discussion between the Anglican Churches of the British Isles and the Lutheran Churches of the Scandinavian and Baltic countries has led to the Porvoo Agreement.

When it met in Lima in 1982, as well as receiving the Lima Report, the Faith and Order Commission of the WCC initiated a new theological programme for the next period. This was entitled 'Towards a Common Expression of the Apostolic Faith Today'. In 1987 the Faith and Order Secretariat published a provisional form of the study document *Confessing One Faith*, and offered it for comment. These comments were studied in their turn and the Standing Commission at its meeting in Dunblane in 1990 approved and authorized a new version of the document *Confessing One Faith*.

The new version of *Confessing One Faith* takes the Nicene Creed as its basic text and offers an explanation of the apostolic faith based on this credal form. In its introduction to the book the Commission notes that

> *the so-called 'non-credal' churches have been particularly sensitive to the dangers of the credal formulas. These formulas easily degenerate into formalism. They may also be misused when their acceptance is enforced upon persons, thus violating their consciences.*

Nevertheless, in assuming that they share the apostolic faith expressed in the Nicene Creed, it is hoped that, at least on special occasions, representatives of these 'non-credal' churches can join in the profession of the Nicene Creed as a witness to their communion in the faith of the 'one, holy, catholic and apostolic church'.[14]

Confessing One Faith is not intended to represent a consensus or even a convergence document. Rather, it is intended to promote and encourage discussion and so play some part in enabling the churches to express the faith together and agree together how wide the boundaries of that faith can be. Once more we are in the position of deciding whether agreement on the faith can be a wide river or needs to be a narrow stream.

The commentary in the book certainly leaves scope for some of the 'David Jenkins' questions. For example, in the section of comment on the words 'and was incarnate from the virgin Mary' we read:

> *Some Christians today feel difficulties with the affir-mation of Mary's virginity. For some, this is because they consider that such a miraculous birth would be inconsistent with God's way of acting towards his peo-ple. Others do not reject in principle the possibility of God's miraculous action. But they do not find in the New Testament any evidence other than the infancy narratives, whose literary form does not necessarily imply a historical claim concerning Mary's virginity. The point of these narratives, they say, is to affirm the divine origin and sonship of Jesus Christ, without specifying the manner in which the incarnation has been realised.[15]*

This study on the faith ran parallel with another study on *The Unity of the Church and the Renewal of Human Community*. This was important because it highlighted other important aspects of belief, such as the position of women, which do not form part of the discussion on the creeds. Some of these issues will be considered later in this chapter.

Some of the questions raised in discussion of the apostolic faith and the nature of visible unity were taken up again at the

Canberra Assembly of the WCC in 1991. The report of the Programme Policy Committee reads:

> *The unity of the church is not something we create but a gift of God which we should receive humbly, promote responsibly and enjoy gratefully. Our common commitment to the fundamentals of the Christian faith continues to call and hold us together . . . The Holy Spirit calls us to acknowledge the unity that exists amongst us and to overcome all barriers in order to be able to share our gifts and ministries while on our common spiritual journey towards visible unity.*[16]

This journey was continued at the Faith and Order Conference in 1993 at Santiago de Compostela, an ancient place of pilgrimage. The Message issued after the conference contained the following words:

> *Concrete challenges stand before the churches. In relation to faith the churches must continue to explore how to confess our common faith in the context of the many cultures and religions, the many social and national conflicts in which we live. Such confession emphasiszes the need for a deeper understanding of the Church and its apostolic character in the light of the holy scriptures.*[17]

The challenge of Santiago has been taken up by the member churches of the WCC and also by national and regional ecumenical bodies.

The concept of the atonement

In June 1997 in Graz, Austria, the second European Ecumenical Assembly took place with the theme 'Reconciliation – Gift of God and Source of New Life'. This Assembly was organized jointly by the Conference of European Churches (CEC), which includes as members the Protestant, Orthodox and Anglican Churches of Europe, and the Council of Roman Catholic Bishops' Conferences of Europe (CCEE). The Assembly also had issues of the visible unity of the Church firmly on its agenda. The background paper which was eventually agreed states:

> *Any reflection on the ecumenical situation must begin by remembering the commandment of our common Saviour, to make visible to the world that communion, which according to the Holy Scriptures and all Christian confessions, is formed by God the Father, Son and Holy Spirit together. Faith in God the Three in One, which we confess at baptism, is the precious, firm bond which holds us together in real community, beyond all divisions, though imperfect because of them. This already existing unity must be expressed publicly and given visible form.[18]*

The key text for this great assembly was 2 Corinthians 5.19:

> *God was in Christ reconciling the world to himself, no longer holding people's misdeeds against them, and has entrusted us with this message of reconciliation.*
> *(Revised English Bible)*

Even this text about reconciliation can, however, be a source of disagreement. The text raises the issue of how we are reconciled to God by the death of Jesus. My evangelical friends in the Church of England would have no problem at all about this. They would say that we are saved by the once-for-all sacrifice of Christ on the cross. This is a concept that they are determined should be included in the eucharistic prayers of the revised *Alternative Service Book*. At the other end of the spectrum of the Church of England, we have the Catholic wing striving to get the concept of eucharistic sacrifice into the eucharist prayer. There is a division of ideas here, but there is also a basic agreement that the death of Jesus on the cross was a sacrifice offered to his Father. The difference in thought lies in whether the sacrifice was offered once and for all or whether it can in some sense be re-enacted in the Eucharist. I have to admit to having difficulty with both concepts, because I have a huge problem with the very idea of Jesus having to offer a sacrifice to God to save us. What kind of God demands a blood offering in this way? It is an idea which horrifies many Christian feminist writers. They might be amused or surprised to discover the concept arouses much feeling amongst Orthodox theologians too.

Before we go any further with this, let us trace the concept back to the beginning. In the second letter to the Corinthians, St Paul does not attempt to answer the question of how the death of Jesus on the cross achieved reconciliation with God. He is content just to proclaim it as truth. Even in some parts of the New Testament, however, attempts were made to answer that question. The letter to the Hebrews, for example, explains the death of Jesus as a once for all sacrifice; but to whom was the sacrifice offered? To God? But why? As the years went by, Christian thinkers tried increasingly to explain how and why. The sacrifice of Jesus was explained as being offered to satisfy God's honour, preserve God's justice or maintain God's holiness.

In the West the sacrifice was more and more presented in legal and juridical terms of satisfaction, compensation, ransom. St Anselm, for example, spoke of God's honour needing to be satisfied, of Christ offering satisfaction on behalf of a humanity that was unable to make up for its disobedience. Other thinkers explained it in terms of Christ dealing with the devil – paying a ransom price to the devil or tricking the devil with his Godhead hidden under his humanity, like fish hook under a worm!

Many of these explanations I find repulsive, even blasphemous. Dr Frances Young, however, in a lecture to a Conference on Reconciliation called by the Conference of European Churches (CEC) in Belgrade, pointed out that some of the theories do have a validity which we must not lose. She linked St Anselm's theory of God's honour needing to be satisfied to a story of her sons throwing stones and breaking a neighbour's windows in a building they thought was deserted. She and her husband had felt obliged to apologize and send a gift of chocolates.

She continued:

> *Pondering this case, we can identify the presence of
> guilt, shame and repentance on the part of the perpetra-*

65

tor (at least once the misdeed was recognized – the boy was innocent of the full implications when he did it). We can see how essential it was that reparation be made, otherwise responsibility was not acknowledged and reconciliation impossible. But we can also see that, the perpetrator being incapable of providing reparation, it had to be provided by someone else.[19]

In spite of this, I still have problems with those who stress the sacrificial nature of Christ's death and God's need to have some sacrifice made to him before he could forgive. According to this view the death of Christ changed God – made a difference to him. He needed the once-for-all sacrifice before he could forgive. I just cannot accept this. Such a view seems to me to be blasphemous, distorted and unbiblical.

What the death of Jesus upon the cross makes startlingly clear is what has been true about God from the beginning – his suffering and redeeming love. To create is to love and to love is to open oneself to suffering. In creating us by an outpouring of his love and giving us free will, God opened himself to great suffering. In his 'all knowledge', God knew that we would sin. In his 'all wisdom', God was ready to deal with that through his own suffering and redeeming love.

In his second Lent lecture in 1994, entitled 'God in the Mess', Bishop David Jenkins wrestled with these issues. He said:

For me, Jesus is the clinching and convincing demonstration of the compassion of God.

That is to say, in Jesus' life and teaching, passion and death, He personally lives out and demonstrates that God is with us in the passion of love and longing. This means that God is involved in the suffering caused by the evil passions which distort, thwart and seem to deny the passions of love and justice. God does not distance Himself from these struggles and sufferings, as if He were presiding from some remote throne. He is to be found in the very struggle and cost

of overcoming evil and non-sense . . . God is in the
midst of the mess, working to redeem His purposes and
promises of passionate love out of all that threatens and
denies it.[20]

The thought which I have expressed and which David Jenkins
puts so much more vividly is shared in their own way by the
Orthodox in their theology. The Orthodox never developed the
juridical approach which occurred in the West. They always believed that, in spite of their sin, human beings still kept something of the image of God and were open to salvation.

In a recent paper published by the Study Committee of CEC,
Bishop Jeremias, an Orthodox bishop from Poland, put it like
this:

Orthodox theology continued the classical approach
developed in the early church.

Reconciliation must not be separated from salva-
tion. Life is reconciled fellowship with God. Christ's
victory leads to the divinization of humankind
(theosis). According to patristic tradition God became
a person so that persons can become God . . .

A juridically oriented interpretation of reconcilia-
tion gained ground in the West, Christ's work of salva-
tion taking on the character of compensation, or
satisfaction. The work of atonement was in danger of
turning into payment for the debt of sin. Passion, mys-
ticism and the scholastic doctrine of satisfaction cast a
shadow on the soteriological motif of the early Church,
which had recognised God's love and mercy as being
responsible for redemption and reconciliation.

In the present situation we would like to avoid any
of the onesidedness of theological history. The cross
event has to be seen in its salvific, incarnational and
cosmological context. Only in a holistic perspective do
we discover reconciliation as a 'gift of God and a
source of new life'.[21]

My Orthodox evangelical friends might be surprised that Orthodox theology of the atonement is nearer to feminist views or the ideas of David Jenkins than to theirs. The 'simple faith' is rather elusive!

Women and unity in believing

At the Ecumenical Assembly in Graz, the delegates spent the mornings revising various documents and formulating recommendations. The participants had a much more exciting time attending workshops or visiting the agora, the peace centre, the women's centre or the ecumenical village.

In the afternoons the delegates and participants met together in so called Dialogue Fora, which centred around the various issues into which consideration of the basic theme of reconciliation had been divided. The first of these was 'The Visible Unity of the Church' and the largest percentage of people opted for this section. The meetings were therefore held in the plenary hall.

I had been the co-moderator of the group preparing the Dialogue Fora on this issue. We decided that we would start off gently with 'Walking Together', bringing in the idea of ecumenical pilgrimages as well as other ways of co-operation. Then we would move on to 'Talking Together' and have some discussions about the official and unofficial dialogues between churches and their implementation in things like the Porvoo Agreement. On the second day we would move into the more difficult areas – the 'healing of memories', with examples from Ireland and the struggle between the Orthodox and the Greek Catholics, and then 'Reconciling the Broken Community of Women and Men in the Church'. On the third day we would deal with the tricky issue of 'Mission/Proselytism and Eucharistic Sharing'.

Half the planning group comprised members from the CEC Churches and the other half were Roman Catholics. The Dialogue Fora went through many stages of planning and acceptance, but at the final stage the hierarchy of CCEE refused to allow the inclusion of the dialogue on 'Reconciling the Broken

Unity in Believing

Community of Women and Men in the Church'. They would not admit that there was any problem and, even if there was, it had nothing to do with the visible unity of the Church and certainly nothing to do with unity in faith.

The staff of CEC fought hard to save this Dialogue Forum. In the end a compromise was reached. The Forum was slightly renamed and banished to the Women's Centre, which was housed in a church in the town at some distance from the Messe where the main Assembly events took place.

It was very sad indeed that the Roman Catholic hierarchy could not see that the issue of the broken community of women and men in the Church is inextricably bound up with issues of visible unity. How can the churches manifest a visible unity to the world, when right at its heart they are deeply divided by the basic human sin of sexism?

Men and women are both made in the image of God and yet throughout its history the Church has regarded women as expendable, second-class citizens – inferior to male human beings.

It is there in the writings of the Fathers of the Church. Tertullian described women as 'the devil's gateway'. Clement of Alexandria thought that the very awareness of their own nature must arouse a sense of shame in women. Jerome castigated women for their sexual appeal in letter after letter. Aquinas spelt out their so-called biological inferiority. Even St Francis maintained that 'intercourse with women was a vain toy', while at the same time feeling an 'ardent devotion to the Mother of Christ'.

Behind some of this lay the Bible. Paul urged women to be silent and respectful and used Genesis 2 to teach that women are dependent on men and must be submissive to them. Perhaps it is spelt out best by an unknown author in the letter to Timothy 2:12–14:

> I do not permit women to teach or dictate to the men; they should keep quiet. For Adam was created first, and Eve afterwards; moreover it was not Adam who was deceived; it was the woman who, yielding to deception, fell into sin.   (REB)

Ecumenical Decade – Churches in Solidarity with Women

In 1988 the WCC launched an Ecumenical Decade – Churches in Solidarity with Women.

The aims of the Decade were to encourage the role of women in decision–making and to value women's insights in spirituality, theology and peace making. During the Decade there has been added the whole issue of violence against women. In the second half of the Decade, team visits have been made to member churches to evaluate its effects. Many of the teams were horrified to discover how the Bible was being used to keep women in an inferior position and even to justify physical violence against them.

The final summary report of the team visits, entitled *Living Letters*, contains the following statement:

> *In one church we heard clergy say they would be opposed to violence 'except in certain circumstances'. One church leader spoke of 'disciplining' his wife and being 'thanked' by her later. Several others queried the definition of 'violence', wanting to distinguish between violence that resulted in death, and 'just hitting'.* [22]

Biblical arguments were also used to oppose the ordination of women or to argue that where women are ordained, it is right that they should not hold positions of real authority. Again there seems to be the same faulty theology underlying all these forms of oppression. It is a faulty theology which just does not recognize that women are made in the image of God as fully as men.

The Deputy General Secretary of the WCC, the Revd Dr Wesley Ariarajah, was so horrified by all this that he wrote a small book entitled *Did I Betray the Gospel? The Letters of Paul and the Place of Women*. In this he tries to deal with the particular texts on women but also to handle the basic issue of how we use and interpret the Bible today, in the light of modern scholarship and changed social conditions.

The things described do not just belong to countries far way. Many women in Britain suffer violence even in the Church, as the research of the Revd Dr Lesley Macdonald has shown. In the Methodist Church, although women have been ordained for over twenty years, they do not feel fully accepted or that their talents are fully used. In the Church of England, ordained women feel betrayed by the Act of Synod and affronted by the 'Flying Bishops', who peddle a theology of taint.

Wrong believing does affect lives. The trouble is, who decides what is right or wrong? In this whole question of unity of belief, where does the truth lie? It is not simple, but it is a search from which we cannot shy away.

Concepts of God

We also need to be able to accept new ideas and recover old ones which have been pushed away by the patriarchal form in which the Christian religion has developed. In Western theology and in almost all liturgies, God is described in masculine terms. In hymns and prayers, strong masculine images are used for God. More and more women and men are becoming dissatisfied with this – even if we are still in the minority. The small book *The Motherhood of God*, published by the Saint Andrew Press in 1984, lists in the appendix many biblical passages in which God is referred to in 'motherly ' terms or in language or imagery which can be described as ' feminine', even if the use of that word may sometimes reflect stereotypes. We have to begin by using the fullness of the biblical imagery to describe God instead of just a tight selection. Then we have to be bold enough to consider whether some of the 'feminine' imagery, even the 'goddess' im-agery, which was suppressed by the writers and proclaimers of truth in the Old Testament, might not legitimately be recovered and used to describe more fully the Being of God who encom-passes and transcends the male and the female.

In 1996, the Women's Communication Centre published re-search material on 'What Women Want' – material obtained by a vast number of postcard questions and answers. The replies about 'religion' showed a deep longing for the feminine in God and a deep dissatisfaction with conventional religion. We ignore this longing at our peril. If the churches cannot satisfy these religious longings, then more and more people will turn to 'New Age' ideas and new religious cults. The whole public reaction to the death of Diana, Princess of Wales, gives us much food for thought. Thousands of people with little time for the Church used religious symbols – candles, lights and flowers – to express their grief. I went down the Mall the Tuesday after her death. It was heavy with the scent of flowers. Those waiting to lay their flowers in front of Buckingham Palace did so in a silence that was palpable. Any consideration of 'Unity in Believing' must take this phenomenon into account.

Called to be One

On a more mundane level, for some years now Churches Together in England (CTE) have been pursuing a programme entitled 'Called to be One', which has attempted to explore the kind of unity we seek. At the CTE Forum held at Swanwick in July 1997, the answers of the churches were discussed and a way ahead suggested. In the final statement from the Forum we find these words:

> *Our unity in mission demands a common life. For very many of us this would find visible expression through: the profession, in word and deed, of the one apostolic faith, which is uniquely revealed in the Holy Scripture and witnessed to in the historic creeds, the sharing of one baptism and the celebrating of one eucharist, a common ministry of word and sacrament, a common ministry of oversight, a means of consulting one another and reaching decisions together.*
>
> *There are others of us who do not share this understanding of visible unity. All of us, however, are committed to travelling together as closely as we can, rejoicing in our diversity without imposing uniformity. The search for visible unity cannot be divorced*

from, or set in opposition to, obedience to the call to share in the mission of God to all humanity.[23]

What was said at the CTE Forum has also been expressed in different ways in the other nations of these islands – Scotland, Wales and Ireland. Indeed, in Wales with its Covenant, and Scotland with the discussion between the churches, even more progress has been made on the way to unity than in England. Such unity is vital, both to fulfil the prayer of our Lord that we may be one and also to give credibility to our witness in the world. In this search for unity, unity in believing has a vital place. This has come out time and time again in this chapter in statements by ecumenical bodies and in the desire of Christians to be one in faith and practice.

What this chapter has also shown is that such unity in belief is not easy to achieve or even to define. What kind of unity in belief do we seek? I have suggested that it must be a broad river of belief and not a narrow stream. It must allow room for a great diversity, as there was diversity already in the New Testament. It must, however, have a common core of faith in Jesus in whom we see revealed the eternal, creative, suffering love of God. Within the being of God is contained power and vulnerability, the masculine and the feminine and more. Before God, we can only kneel in wonder and our faith must be expressed in creeds which are songs of joy and not tests of orthodoxy or means of oppression.

As Metropolitan John of Pergamum put it at the Faith and Order Conference in Santiago, 'The Creed is not there for theologians to study, but for communities to sing.'[24]

NOTES

1. 'Good God', Lecture 1: 'God in the Beginning'; Bishop of Durham's Lent Lectures 1994, published in pamphlet form, p.11.
2. Ibid., p.14.
3. David J. A. Clines, *The Theme of the Pentateuch* (JSOT Supplemental Series 10; Sheffield Academic Press).
4. James D. G. Dunn, *Unity and Diversity in the New Testament* (second edition; SCM Press, London and Trinity Press International, Philadelphia, 1990), p.5.

5. Ibid., p.6.
6. Ibid., p.30.
7. Ibid., p.31.
8. Ibid., p.228.
9. Ibid., p.230.
10. Frances Young, *The Making of the Creeds* (SCM Press, London and Trinity International Press, Philadelphia, 1991), p.3.
11. Ibid., p.5.
12. Ibid., p.13.
13. Ibid., p.15.
14. *Confessing One Faith* (Faith and Order Paper No. 153; WCC, Geneva, 1991), p. 4.
15. Ibid., pp.53–4.
16. Michael Kinnamon (ed.), *Signs of the Spirit* (Report of the Seventh Assembly of the WCC, Report of the Programme Policy Committee; WCC, Geneva, 1991), p.186.
17. Thomas Best and Gunther Gassmann (eds.), *On the Way to Fuller Koinonia* (Report of the Fifth World Conference on Faith and Order, The Message; WCC, Geneva, 1993), p.227.
18. Second European Ecumenical Assembly (EEA2), *Final Document* No. 3 (Background to the Recommendations for Action, 'The Search for Visible Unity in the Church'), p.7.
19. *Reconciliation in a Theological Dimension.* Paper given by Professor Frances Young at the Ecumenical Dialogue on Reconciliation, Belgrade, 19–22 February 1996 (Conference of European Churches, Geneva), p. 28.
20. David Jenkins, 'God in the Mess' (Bishop of Durham's Lent Lectures 1994), pp.10–11.
21. Pamphlet entitled *Reconciliation in Europe – Theological, Ecumenical and Ethical Aspects* (Conference of European Churches Study Committee, Iasi, Roumania), p.4.
22. *Living Letters: A Report of Visits to the Churches during the Ecumenical Decade of Churches in Solidarity with Women* (WCC, Geneva, 1997), p.26.
23. Statement issued by the Forum of Churches Together in England (Swanwick, Derbyshire, July 1997), p. 2.
26. Comment by Metropolitan John (Zizioulas) of Pergamum quoted in the broadsheet of information about the Fifth World Conference on Faith and Order (CCBI, 1993), p.1.

Four

GO OUT AND GET LEARNING!
Martin Conway

> *Jesus replied, 'The most important commandment is this, "Listen, Israel! The Lord our God is the only Lord. Love the Lord your God with all your heart, with all your soul, with all your mind, and with all your strength." The second most important commandment is this: "Love your neighbour as you love yourself." '*
> (Mark 12.29–31, quoting Deuteronomy 6.4ff, GNB)

> *The gloriousness of God breaks through and beyond the syntax of any of our languages.*
> (Maxwell Craig's Introduction to this book, paraphrased by Martin Conway)

What is so central about education?

Why should a book like this have a chapter on education? Above all, because Jesus commanded all those who would follow him to love God with their minds, indeed all their minds, as much as with every other dimension of their being.

More generally, a study of what Christian unity could mean in practice is bound to include a central emphasis on the educational challenge. For whoever says 'one' about God is also speaking of what that leads us to mean by 'all' and 'whole' in a vast range of contexts. Education is nothing if not the process by which any individual person, any human team or community, indeed any tribe or nation, grows into awareness of their participation in a wider and richer whole. It enables us to share in the fruits of a human interdependence that goes far back into history

75

and reaches across the geographical, political and cultural boundaries of today, providing insight and inspiration by which to explore the possibilities now being set before us by the one God.

It is widely accepted that the 21st century will enable, indeed require, a much higher level of education in many more of us than the 20th has seen, not only for the sake of the sheer survival of the human race, but also so that humanity can learn to deal wisely with the opportunities coming towards us over the horizons of knowledge and skill.

At the same time it deserves to be equally commonplace that one of the most promising dimensions of living as disciples of Jesus of Nazareth is that the Holy Spirit gives his followers gifts by which – to conflate Ephesians 3 and 4 – Christians may grow up in every way into Christ. We are not called to stay as we happen to be, but to grow, and grow together, into the breadth and length, the height and depth of Christ's love, which can never be fully known beforehand. The promised maturity comes as a Christian and a church, in and for whatever their situation and obedience may prove to be, reach out in a unity of faith and knowledge to the very height of Christ's full stature, and are completely filled with the very nature of God.

This is not, of course, for our own sake or as any kind of separate, privileged status, but simply as those called and enabled for service of whomever God gives us as neighbours.

No, Jesus was not a 'highly educated person' in the sense of having a string of degrees or professional qualifications. But he shows us the way in at least three key respects:

• he had learned to know and to be able to interpret his people's scriptures with an always original and challenging freshness;
• he was a remarkably whole person in his relationships, showing in the various episodes of his life an integrity that cannot be separated out into 'competences', 'knowledge', 'morality', 'sensitivity' and 'religion' as if those are separate or can be seen and practised in isolation from each other;
• he was invariably open to whichever people came around him,

because he was no less invariably open to the purposes and intentions of God.

Here's hoping that each of you who read this has discovered in your own experience of 'education' enough of wider horizons opening up and deeper sensitivities coming to be of crucial importance to your own relationships, that you can believe in education as a key instrument for the future God holds open for humanity, and have not had to suffer it as the imposition of other people's agendas, turning it into an unwelcome prison.

Education and the contemporary ecumenical movement

Let's backtrack for a moment. This book is mostly about dimensions of the ecumenical movement, a phenomenon largely of the twentieth century – the century, as Bishop Lesslie Newbigin once said, which has been the first for at least 1500 years to have seen more effort put into the healing of quarrels between Christians than into the creation and maintenance of divisions.

In these efforts, those involved have learned that their divisions are never purely 'inter-church affairs'; they also reflect, and have all too often helped to strengthen, divisions between wider human groupings – of class, ethnic identity, nationality etc.

We have also learned that the healing of divisions between Christians requires a long-term repentance and perseverance, both in facing up to the quarrels by which churches became divided and in seeking health and mutual affirmation in the life of the community and the world at large. Christ calls and empowers his Church invariably to pursue what is right for its 'own life' as a contribution to what God wants for humankind as a whole, in other words, for the unity of the human family.

One humanity?

One humanity – yes, a natural consequence of faith in one God, in one creation by his love, and in one under-arching framework of reliable truth and meaning in this world. These 'unities' – the abstract noun is always inadequate ! – hang together, and each has an 'all' and a 'whole' built into it too.

One God?

That God is one and sovereign over all things is the heart of the faith of Jews, Christians and Muslims alike, even if each tradition has its own priorities and expressions for interpreting this basic fact. It matters more than anything else, Jews, Christians and Muslims traditionally believe, to be able to claim a single origin for all that is, and a single end towards which all reality is called. Without this, life cannot avoid being pulled in different and clashing directions, as it so often is anyway by our own choosing. Without it, no Jew, Christian or Muslim can feel confident about seeking agreement for bridging or healing the constant disputes and divisions between us.

Yet, of course, this can never be more than a claim of faith: there is no way of proving it, of imposing it on people who for whatever reason cannot see the truth in it. This is no accident, for it is one of the joy-enhancing mysteries of God that the creation has been so fashioned that it allows for an amazing degree of free will, free choice and free use of power by human beings. God rules over all in a self-chosen mode of encouraging and promoting mutuality in freedom with and among the creatures who are mind- and spirit-endowed. God does not just create and then leave us to it – as it often feels like – but is eternally involved in 'letting creatures be' in a strong and positive sense that is often interpreted in images close to 'education'.

Christians have spoken of this life as a vale of soul-making, a testing-ground, a preparation for the life to come. Seen in a negative light as if what goes on here in the created order is entirely secondary and doomed to something near failure, these images can sound disheartening, even gloomy. Seen, however, positively – and how could a loving God/Father be anything but positive about a world into which God/Son was sent? – education is a natural process by which human beings learn to make sense of this complex and infinitely intricate planet. Is not the challenge to discover how best all creatures can live together, in fulfilment of the possibilities built into each and every one, the most exciting and encouraging purpose to which our distinctive talents as human beings can be put?

One creation?

Yet in fact, of course, we human beings are more likely to make a wretched mess of things, in matters of environmental concern as much as in our social and indeed personal relationships. This is why Jews and Christians speak of 'original sin', awareness of which is one of the positive, indeed hopeful, dimensions of our faith. The truth of that phrase lies not in human beings using the powers given us, but in supposing that it is we who determine what is good and what is evil, and so make ourselves into gods, presuming to run the universe for our own benefit rather than for all creatures and for the real God/creator.

In regard to social and personal relationships, many people have learned to realize how badly we behave to one another, and to have at least some idea of how to try again with hope of improvement. So in these last decades some people are collectively beginning to understand why the environmental mess is so bad and how we might – just might, given sufficient mutual agreement and common will – be able to provide the planet with a chance to restore itself to something significantly nearer health.

Part of what we have begun to learn is a vivid respect for the range of diversity (bio-diversity in the jargon) in nature. One of the threats being heightened by much unthinking action is a diminution of this diversity, leading to a severe reduction in the range of potential contributions to our collective future.

This in turn is equally true in the social as well as the environmental context: the degree of mutual inter-racial and inter-cultural learning that today's multi-peopled cities open up is – for all the difficulties experienced by those accustomed to living among only 'our own sort' – a vivid promise of how much richer life will be when we can all benefit from a wider range of human potentialities. On our doorsteps or in a neighbouring continent, the wide range of diversity among human beings is nothing strange to any TV watcher – whether it be the languages people speak, or their distinctive cultures, abilities, intuitions, expectations and much more. And yet we are all equally aware that the human species as a whole is one, that all human peoples belong together, with powers and in-built instincts that are deeply common, however various our use of them.[1]

Today's problem with this way of speaking lies in the wider reaches of the universe, beyond our immediate planet. Looking out into the unimaginable extent of space, we hardly know how our words can begin to ring 'true' to realities so distant and unknown. Yet the very fact that we can begin to send intricate lumps of metal to start on quite new possibilities of exploration is a sign that we are going to have to work on the meaning of 'truth' and 'error', not as ours, but as an essential judgement that God gives us to use, for the stars and planets just as much as we already use it for the familiar aspects of God's one creation.

And a multi-cultural society?

As I have suggested above, the arguments here in Britain over whether or not we wish to be a 'multi-cultural society' represent a vital piece of social education, and one which is going on under many diverse pressures in almost every part of the world. Countries like Brazil and South Africa boast of being 'rainbow societies' which have now learned, or are at least trying hard to learn, how to be fair to people of different ethnic backgrounds among their citizens. Yugoslavia has provided the entire world with a crass example of nationalisms rejecting and refusing one another, and so ruining each other's chances. Running sores of tribal intransigence in Ireland, Sri Lanka, Palestine and many other areas remind us how easy it is to fall back into certainties that have not yet become unlearned as people confront the challenge to choose a 'new way' involving two and more peoples rather than just 'our own'.

As someone who has had the privilege of living in Birmingham for ten years, possibly the most multi-racial and multi-faith of Britain's major cities, I will gladly witness to both how much effort it takes for a city to make the most of such diversities of culture and expectations among its communities, and how much purpose and joy in working for the common future can be discovered when that sort of effort is encouraged into reality.[2]

There are delicate balances to be explored and respected, for instance between the ways in which a 'majority' culture wishes to express itself and those in which various 'minorities' may find it appropriate to express their specific and different senses of identity and self-affirmation. Moreover, in a city where there are now some three generations of Muslims, Sikhs and Hindus living among an Anglo-Irish 'majority', each with a markedly different attitude to 'British' culture and the educational patterns considered normal in it, any such balances have to be held both sensitively and flexibly. Allowance needs to be made for the constant shifting in expectations concerning both the separate and the common identities. Respect for another's identity-line is always a basic courtesy. For any one of us, especially someone identified with 'the majority', to delineate another's identity, let alone a community's, will almost always be wrong!

One under-arching truth?

The wider the range of traditions and communities present in a city or local area, the more care needs to be put into exploring and expressing a provisional common framework of truth and meaning. Things that any one tradition regards as self-evident prove to be much more disputed in another. Yet the great majority of believers in Birmingham, for example, have learned to regard the identification of an under-arching framework as both possible and indeed necessary. This gives us something by which we can together look into the implications of the city's, and the nation's, policies with good hope that we can discover a basis for, say, an overall policy for religious education in highly mixed schools.

Perhaps the single most vital thing to be said in the early stages is that any such exploration will be far better done among those who have already become friends than among a group who have not yet learned to respect and enjoy one another. Christians should be among the first to recognize this, for our experience is that one can only share good news with those who already regard the sharer as a friend to be trusted.

Renewing and reshaping the Church into a learning community

The main and overall conclusion I draw from these faith claims is that Christ has from the beginning called his Church to serve as a 'learning community', eager to learn and to share that capacity with all those around it, in a way that too many Christians in our part of the world have seemed to overlook in recent centuries. Maxwell Craig gets it precisely right in his Introduction when he says: *'The glory of God breaks the syntax of our language'*.

At the beginning of this chapter I paraphrase his first words as 'God's gloriousness' to emphasize how much this is a dimension of everything we know about God rather than one element among others. Our 'learning' needs to involve a lot more of life than what we find in school books. I also risk paraphrasing his 'breaks the syntax' into a breaking 'through and beyond', to emphasize the positive and hopeful rather than only the destructive and painful, if often necessary, side of this breaking. And rather than only one language I paraphrase 'any of our languages' because it is the multiplicity of them, many expressed in gestures and ways of acting, as well as words, that matters. While I am thus wholly with Maxwell in agreeing that no single culture can expect to grasp God adequately in our feeble words, I have come to rejoice in the fact that other people's languages, and still more other people's cultural sensitivities, will often be able to help us tread together more surely where your language or mine gives out.

As that glory breaks through one level of our awareness, so the surprising promise of deeper and more glorious levels of awareness shines through. To be a learning community is to be called to advance from one range of perceptions to another. This is by no means only a tough and determined struggle, though it may well at times involve this. There are indeed some things – the Arabic language for instance – which no British person can learn without hard and persevering work. But then there are others – African rhythms, for instance – which it is sheer joy to get into one's bloodstream! Overall, learning is as enjoyable for adults as it is in a primary school, especially if it opens up possibilities of awareness and friendship previously beyond our grasp.

Think for a moment how this emphasis on a 'learning community' could transform one or two familiar aspects of the Church's life.

Pastoral visiting

As church members and pastors who go around visiting people, especially the sick or lonely, we would go not just to offer companionship and comfort, valuable though those are, but also to tap into their wisdom and to learn from their experiences. Even a conversation directly about that person's present difficulties could at best help the visitor to see how society might be able to handle such difficulties more creatively. The result of a pastoral visit for the visitor should not be coming away with a sense of 'duty done', but seeing more that deserves to be shared in other appropriate quarters in the Church and in society.

Sunday worship

A striking renewal of worship has been experienced in the major conferences of the World Council of Churches in the past fifteen years. One of its glories has been the recovered expectation of excitement in acts of worship that open hearts and minds in new ways. For the WCC has found ways for all the participants to learn new things and so glorify God more truly and lastingly.

This is not primarily due to good preaching (worthwhile though that certainly is!), but to simple devices such as providing time and occasion for people to introduce themselves to those who happen to be next to them and discuss a key issue in the service; or using at least one new song or prayer from a minority tradition, so that in learning to worship through it most participants will enlarge their musical, spiritual and cultural horizons. Even planning worship in a way that expects everyone to do something original (suggest a prayer or risk drawing a picture, etc.) and share it with a neighbour can bring about innumerable surprises and new friendships. How often do we return home from worship on a Sunday thrilled by some new awareness or discovery?

A world-wide fellowship

In Birmingham, as in meetings of the World Council of Churches, it is relatively commonplace to find yourself sitting in church next to someone of a different skin colour and language. Even this simple fact brings to life the affirmation in the Apostles' Creed of 'one holy, catholic (Luther translated it as 'universal') Church' – the promise that the Church of Jesus' followers would be made up of many more than 'our own sort'. As a world-wide fellowship the Church is committed to praying for Christ's many members across all barriers, enriching and empowering one another for the daily confrontation with the relative, but always dangerous, powers of this world. But how often do we actively seek to draw that prayer, that wealth of cultures and that power of discipleship into our own experience?

The Ecumenical Prayer Cycle launched by the WCC nearly twenty years ago[3] had the potential, according to my then boss Harry Morton, to revolutionize the hearts and political and economic wills of Christians in a Britain conditioned to think of itself as superior. By praying each week in partnership with Christians of another country, and so learning something of the great challenges they face and how they respond to them, we would inevitably see our own situations in a new light. This can happen simply through language. Making use of not only Hebrew Hallelujahs and Greek Kyrie Eleisons but also Swahili Mungus and Indonesian Tuhans in our worship gives a sense of the power and joy of a fellowship that overcomes barriers of language and economic 'development' in mutual joy.

Is it this sense of global worship which is helping us to inspire the campaigns to convince European supermarkets to buy fairly traded goods, and to pressurize oil firms into taking seriously the social consequences of their drilling and plundering of the earth's long-stored mineral wealth? There is plenty more to share and learn in this way if Christians are to tackle in God's name the 'manic logic of global capitalism',[4] including the crying shame of Third World debt and the crying scandals of the world's arms trade.

Inter-generational learnings

The syntaxes that God's glory will help us to break through also include those of the ever-growing generation gaps in a society flooded by constant changes and novelties. Many local churches now actively make the most of having children in the worshipping community, and learn with and from them in one part of the main act of Sunday worship, so perhaps the time has come for youth groups to share their concerns and discoveries more regularly and normally with the older people in a congregation.

In a world where, as Margaret Mead once put it, 'the over-forties are bound to feel foreigners', it is the sixteen to twenty year olds who can best help their elders break beyond the familiar in order to learn what God may be offering for the years ahead. But so far few churches have learned how to build this into their normal patterns of mutual upbuilding.

We need this upbuilding, of course, not just for the sake of the congregation, but so that the Church as a whole may be empowered to take a share in what we hope will be our society's creative response to the situations confronting older and younger people. For the older these may be the likelihood of loneliness in a mobile society, or increasing mental debility in later years. The younger face the prevalence of unemployment, or reliance on drugs for thrills, or the conditions which cause so many young people to leave home and land themselves in homelessness. The churches cannot expect to have sure-fire 'answers' to any of these problems, but it is clearly important that church members – like their partners in other social groupings – should try to understand as carefully as possible why these conditions are affecting more and more people, and so discern yet better ways of responding, for the sake of society as a whole and the individuals immediately concerned.

Christians in education

I turn now to look rather more narrowly at ways in which Christians in our churches can learn to support the work of those Christians who are professionally involved in the 'world of education', that vast complex of institutions and resources which societies like ours now rely on to train our next generations for the inherently unpredictable world of tomorrow.

If Christ's Church is at heart a learning community, then it is not surprising that a significant proportion of its members are to be found working in schools and colleges. Let it never be forgotten that in Europe the original impetus for many of the basic purposes and patterns of education down the centuries has come from Christians, from the medieval monks to the training in human relations and counselling in our day.

So far, in the name of the one God, I have stressed mutual, active, participatory discovery and widening of horizons that involve both 'students' and 'teachers'. This mutuality remains no less crucial in the specific context of schools and colleges. All education is diminished if it is experienced as the all-competent teacher graciously (let alone otherwise) imparting precious pieces of knowledge to pupils seen as unskilled and ignorant. Our colleagues who serve as teachers need dynamic friendships with people in other 'worlds' to enable them to 'break through the syntax' of their sometimes overly self-preoccupied profession.

More generally, my insistence that awareness of the oneness of God leads into a concern for the wholeness and universality of the creation, deserves in this context to underline a concern for the 'wholeness' of learning.

European culture since Descartes and the Enlightenment has made huge strides by drawing distinctions and focusing on particular realities. Yet many people feel that this has been taken far too far. Not least, there are many in education who fear that the introduction of prescriptive curriculum guidelines in each school subject will break up the experience of learning into a myriad of 'bits' that no one knows how to hold together in a sensible whole – though I understand that Scotland has been pursuing this in a more flexible way than England. Can the churches provide a companionship that constantly puts our professional occupations into the wider context they need?

A complementary dimension of 'wholeness' essential to all education has to do with the child, student and indeed teacher as a 'whole person', and with the development of their relationships. All teachers need to care enough about their students to sense how each as a person is integrating the totality of their learning and what that may suggest to those responsible for the teaching. Can outsiders also find the spiritual energy to care for those coping with the strains of teaching – doubly intense with all the current governmental stress on 'driving up standards' – as 'whole persons' in the sight of God, not only professional cogs in the educational machine? The roles now available in and around schools and colleges as parents, governors, financial supporters, partners in allied professions, etc., deserve high priority for this pastoral reason too.

Alongside the 'whole', there is the 'all'. The pressures on schools and colleges to obey the competitive logic of the adult commercial world make it horribly easy for more attention to be devoted to those likely to succeed than to those whose background or abilities make them more likely to fail the set demands. Fircroft College, Selly Oak, is an educational community devoted to enabling 'those whom the school system failed' – the only qualification for entry is to have *no* school leaving qualification. My experience at Fircroft has taught me just how often that sort of 'failure' is the result of poor teaching methods and/or the criteria of 'success' imposed by the adult world. Fircroft shows in a myriad of different personalities how often the same person, a few or many years later, can enter into the adventure of education with a commitment, zest and indeed creativity that puts many more conventionally 'successful' students to shame.

My wife was persuaded to serve as 'disability officer' for the Selly Oak Colleges, and found herself uncovering a similar concern for patterns of 'inclusive learning'. This phrase points not only to the provision of facilities for students with disabilities – from wheelchair access to computers that can read texts aloud for visually impaired people – but, no less important, to the opening up of awareness in the 'normally abled' of how much they have been losing out by not benefiting from the companionship of colleagues with a different range of sensitivities.

As well as the 'whole' and the 'all', Christians must remain critically concerned for the central question of the purpose and meaning of education, especially in an age when it is constantly seen in functional terms related to specific skills for income-generating work. Not that that concern is to be dismissed, but it too needs to be held in a wider and deeper context. In our mixed and ever-changing societies there can be no question of simply assuming a 'Christian basis' for all schooling. Christians will continue to ground our educational commitments in a faith claim about the all-encompassing creativity of God. But that is no reason to spurn or underestimate the awareness and discoveries of others. Rather than insist on any one expression of fundamental truth, Christians today will seek to ensure a lively and open debate about the deeper and most central questions, in the faith that God the Holy Spirit will be able, through that sort of sharing, to 'lead us into new truth' that can serve God's purposes.

This is for me a lasting ground on which to justify the requirement of the 1944 Education Act in England and Wales that every pupil shall share in 'religious education' that does not 'indoctrinate' in any one faith tradition, and that every school shall hold regular assemblies (whether every day or not is a secondary matter) in which students can share in common acts of worship. Both these provisions are much under fire at present. There needs to be much more discussion about the adequate provision of time in the timetable, and about the in-service training for head teachers in the art of leading assemblies, and specialist teachers for religious education. Even beyond those more detailed aspects of the debate, it seems foolhardy to try to lay down exact requirements in this area, in a country whose 'religious profile' is changing as rapidly and constantly as anything else. Yet it remains vital to try to ensure that the levels of human awareness and commitment that we designate by the imprecise and indefinable word 'religion' are made available to all for exploration and debate.

The disputed question of 'religious schools'

Another topic on which there are continuing and sometimes heated debates, and which must necessarily concern those who believe in one God, is the desirability of provision for separate 'religious schools'. The 1944 Education Act for England and Wales (its provisions for Scotland are in this respect essentially similar) allowed 'church' schools a distinct place in the overall 'state/county' provision. This meant that in England and Wales both the Anglican and Roman Catholic Churches could sponsor their own schools; the Free Churches by and large decided not to take advantage of this provision. Like the Church of Scotland, they chose instead to put their educational commitments into helping to develop the 'state school' system as a whole. So for a generation the Church of England continued to provide a large number of schools, especially in rural areas, and on occasion open new ones, seeing its schools as in principle open to the entire community of the area. The Roman Catholic Church followed a quite different policy of 'Catholic schools for Catholic children', and put enormous efforts into building enough schools for all its children, not always successfully, as its own members moved around the country. A small number of Jewish schools have also benefited from this provision, teaching their own syllabus of religious education, although in at least one case known to me also gladly welcoming children of Christian families into that syllabus. In all three communities there has been, off and on, a measure of debate about the precise purposes and policies of these 'separate' schools, often, of course, prompted by their cost. It would be wrong to suppose that all Anglicans, all Roman Catholics or all Jews see their 'denominational schools' in the same terms. But by and large the 1944 consensus has remained alive and strong.

In the last few years, however, this debate has taken on a new actuality. On the one hand this has been the result of much wider and more sensitive awareness of the situation in Northern Ireland, where the Catholic schools have seemed to most Protestants to be enforcing a separation among children that can only be unhelpful in the search for peace. This has led, for instance, to the 'experiment' of Lagan College as a deliberately inter-church school enjoying the backing of both communities. Still more recently, there is a quite new pressure from within the Muslim community, though by no means backed by all Muslims, for state funding of schools run by other faith communities.

This chapter cannot go into all the detail that this question deserves. Yet it is of vivid interest to those of us committed to discerning the purposes of the one God for the people of God as a whole. It will remain for a generation or two at least one of the key questions in the growth of a genuinely multi-cultural society.

As barely more than an interested observer, I have come to feel that there are perhaps three distinct yet complementary dimensions to a debate in which many more of us need to be sensitively involved. First, we clearly need precisely that kind of long-range and happily open discussion about the central nature and purpose of education in the sight of God that I mentioned in the previous section. In his epoch-making book *Belief in a Mixed Society*, Christopher Lamb suggests that we need to help one another work through the tensions that necessarily arise between those who – for reasons of 'culture' as much as 'faith' (hard as it is to draw the line between them!) – see education in terms of the 'transmission' of inherited wisdom, and those who will focus more on education as enabling a 'transformation' of the future by encouraging the new generation to make its own explorations into what deserves to be understood and done. There will be no easy answers in such a debate, but by paying attention to what the 'other sides' want to say we shall all gain immeasurably in the awareness important for a multi-cultural society.

Second, and rather more straightforward, there is a simple question of natural justice. A country that has allowed any one religious 'denomination' to have funding for its own schools cannot withhold a comparable possibility of funding from another religious community whose members have become citizens. In principle it might be thinkable to try to reshape the educational system in a way that owes no religious bodies any such 'right' – as the 1997 Labour government seems unwittingly to have tried in its first draft of a new Education Act. It backtracked sharply as the churches reacted! Yet with church schools, at least in England, clearly enjoying a popularity often denied to secular schools, any such move could only be even more divisive. So I have no hesitation in saying that, provided of course they measure up to the accepted standards for all schools, the Muslims – and Hindus, Sikhs and Buddhists if they so wish – should be allowed state funding for an appropriate number of schools. This will also enable the rest of us to begin to discover the distinctive qualities that Muslim traditions of education can contribute to British society as a whole.

Third, I suggest that this whole area of debate needs to be seen as passing through different stages, as the various communities in a multi-cultural society learn both to give and receive from their partners of other communities and traditions.

To start with my own 'tradition' – as a member of the Church of England, part of the 'effortless majority' in England – Anglican policy for church schools in England has now reached a stage where the Church takes a pride in doing what it can to provide schools in which church members, as head teachers, governors, teachers of Religious Education and other subjects, can present to pupils the best Christians can offer from whatever background. There have certainly been times in the past when Church of England schools generally kept out students from nonconformist or other 'unsuitable' backgrounds, and no one in today's Church would dare claim that 'our' schools within the state system never practise discrimination of some sort. (The position and policies of the fee-charging independent schools that claim a link with the Church of England is utterly different again.) But the overall policy has developed strongly in the direction of Anglican schools in the common system making available to the population of their area the best education they can, in the belief that this is entirely consistent with Christian obedience.

I remember, for instance, the way Muslim parents in the part of Oxford where I live spoke some years ago about the excellence of the church primary school (of which their children made up 80%) as a place where faith in God was evidently and openly taken seriously throughout all activities. It helped not a little that the then vicar appeared every day in his cassock, evidently loved the children, joked with them, and led prayers in assembly that were addressed to God, but never explicitly 'through Jesus Christ', although everyone knew that this was his personal faith.

A different stage in the pilgrimage of faith was represented in 1944 by the Roman Catholic policy, concerned that 'their own children' should be taught 'their own faith', a faith that by definition could not be adequately set out by any teacher other than 'their own'. From outside, this is bound to look like the policy of a community which feels itself to be in a minority and is defensively concerned to 'protect' its own children. This is probably not so different from the emotions that have led many Muslims in the UK today to plead for the right to have 'their own' schools within the state system. Inasmuch as respect for the particular convictions of the neighbour is a prime commitment of all Christians, one cannot but see this as appropriate, at the point where a recently-arrived community cannot yet trust the 'host community' enough to feel able to work out a common policy in such a sensitive matter as education for children.

The Roman Catholic Church is an eloquent witness to the fact that the pilgrimage of faith always moves people on into new stages. Its 1980 Pastoral Congress began its decision-making by sending a 'loyal message' to the Queen, and went on to press for many new initiatives of partnership with other Christians. Many Catholics that I meet today, whether or not they were themselves brought up in Catholic schools, point to the evidence that a Catholic schooling all too often seems to function as an 'inoculation', providing adult (ex-)Catholics with just enough 'religion' to ensure that they never take it seriously. Such voices are likely to be warmly in favour of 'inter-church schools', of which a number now exist, in which the Anglican and Roman Catholic Churches together provide a school which sets out the best in the all-Christian tradition, without limiting entry to 'their own children'.

It will no doubt be a fair time yet before the British Muslim community at large feels ready for this degree of partnership, but individual voices can be heard warning against the dangers of isolating children and insisting that Muslim schools will want to become active partners with other schools in their area. So, in present practice, my concern is less about the relatively small number of possible Muslim schools than whether there are enough Muslims teaching in the general run of schools, and – still more – whether enough of the 'ordinary' teachers are sufficiently sensitive to the backgrounds and feelings of children from the minority communities to be able to encourage them appropriately.

But I have been glad to note that at least most of those professionally trained as Religious Education teachers have been among the earliest professionals to know how to respond positively and in a health-creating way to the arrival of significant numbers of people of 'other' faiths.[5]

So I believe – another faith claim! – that British society should now welcome the advent of Muslim schools – and indeed Hindu, Sikh and Buddhist schools if those communities wish, although the evidence at present is that they are much more likely to want full integration into the general schools for their children.[6] These 'separate' schools, observing the standards laid down for all schools, will serve precisely as springboards which can, in the relative 'safety' of an 'own approach', prepare tomorrow's British Muslims to launch into the demanding, but also in the long run unusually meaningful and hopeful, adventure of inter-religious pilgrimage. By which point there will surely be patterns of religious education coming over the horizon which few of us can yet see.

A footnote for my colleagues in the inter-Christian ecumenical movement. I am one who has long insisted that the exploration of inter-Christian and inter-church relations is not to be equated with the much newer (at least in Britain – hardly in India!) and inevitably, for the moment, more tentative exploration into the possibilities of inter-religious understanding and co-operation. But the similarities between these two movements, and the fact that for Christians the one undeniably points towards the necessity of also undertaking the other, are also to be warmly affirmed, in education as in other spheres of life in society.

Looking into the twenty-first century

The new century will surely demand that all peoples become more adequately a 'learning species' (as we were created to be) that can both treasure the inherited wisdom of our various traditions and constantly explore with one another how to make the best of new opportunities. That sounds like a mere platitude, yet we actually exemplify and practise it very little in matters of faith.

If I could arrange one innovation overnight, I would ask governments to finance a regular 'learning break' for all adults – say six months every ten years to start with – to be spent in some community and activity that will distinctively enlarge their cap-

94

acities. I suggest this, not because I know precisely how it could be organized, but because I believe it to be of the highest importance, both for the world's good and for the sake of obedience to the intentions of God, that far-reaching new possibilities of education for adults should become available.

There are many different fields in which this is desirable, from training for promotion or for a change of job to the acquisition of second and third languages and looking into dimensions of human living overlooked in earlier learning – the fine arts, for instance, or local history, or searching into the depths of religious truth. Central is the belief – another truth claim! – that each of us is created by the one God to become more than we presently are, a belief that is as true for people with Ph.D.s as for those who have never left the village in which they were born. For human beings were created, so Jews, Christians and Muslims believe, 'in the image of God' – i.e. with inbuilt potential to enter into relationship and co-creatorship with God during this present life and, in the fullness of life in God's coming reign hereafter, to move into the depths of friendship and creativity that God has been exercising since the beginning.

With my experience of working in international organizations and of the inter-cultural training and widening of horizons that the Selly Oak Colleges have been pursuing in recent years, I see these new possibilities most readily in international terms. It has been a deep satisfaction and joy to observe adult Christians and Muslims, for instance, each fully responsible for their own believing and practice, studying, arguing, researching and imagining together in mutual awareness of both faith traditions, in the hope of discovering paths of partnership that can allow both communities to move in faith beyond the many fears and disputes between us.

Can we look to a time, not far off, when adults generally can be expected to be fluent in at least two languages? This would be good not only for the sake of contact between the two peoples involved, but because someone who has learned a second language will have a certain freedom in handling both, and can move between the cultures with a mind prepared for difference and new insight. All to the good if the more adventurous of the British could be encouraged to learn Chinese or Arabic rather than French or Spanish. Good too if British Sign Language could be widely learned in order to open up communication between the hearing-impaired and others. Even better if people in 'majority' communities set themselves to learn 'minority' languages, whether represented in their own area (Urdu and Punjabi in Birmingham, for instance) or from far away. All too many languages, like species of birds or plants, are likely in the years ahead to be swamped, even 'disappeared' – like that of Waiwai's people – by the insensitive power of tomorrow's majorities.

Can we encourage many more young people to spend a year of their education as guests of people in a distinctly different culture? That would give many of them the advantage in mastery of the language concerned; still more, it could open up friendships and a confidence in moving in a different society that would greatly benefit the adults – and with them, the society they come from throughout the years ahead. In small ways, Christians are already pioneering this sort of possibility through world-wide contacts between the churches.

'No peace between the nations without peace between the religions.' Hans Küng's dictum deserves its fame. Can many more of us, as an act of Christian obedience on behalf of our churches at large, give time and effort to exploring how this challenge could be met in our particular spheres of work, our cities, schools and colleges? I remain startled by Wesley Ariarajah's assertion in 1982, when he participated in a team visit by the World Council of Churches to the UK in the year of the Falklands war, that Britain was in an unusually favourable position among the world's nations to explore relations between people of different faiths, because Britain had a relatively full cross-section of all the great world faiths and had long since faced up to (even if by no means fully mastered!) some of the most difficult lessons about tolerance and democracy.

Since then Britain has been fortunate to have known much

inter-religious exploration, but there is obviously a long way to go yet. People involved in all the 'mainline' occupations of society – the bankers, the trade unionists, the exporters, the journalists, the sports crowd – need to be no less active on this way than the theologians and the school teachers. Not forgetting the politicians either: each one of us will know at least one who could profit from spending six months in an Arabic Art College or a Chinese Academy of Social Sciences!

I long for the Christian community to face and respond to the challenge of ensuring that adult education – of many different types – becomes much more readily accepted as a normal part of what we expect of one another, because it reflects what God not only expects but makes possible for us all. Can the agenda of today's world-wide ecumenical movement suggest to the churches in Britain and Ireland ways by which we can pioneer many new openings?

NOTES

1. For a particularly striking and unusual, but heart-warming, example – and a Scottish one at that: see A. T. Campbell, 'Getting to Know Waiwai' (Routledge, London, 1995), in which an outside anthropologist describes his efforts to know and share the world of a tiny tribal community in an endangered part of the Amazon basin. He expounds at some length his painstaking exploration of the unique features of their language, having become aware that even if it is now spoken by no more than a handful of people, it adds an undeniable richness to the known possibilities of human communication.

2. The literature on multi-cultural questions is of course immense. Three recent publications may be worth mentioning for those who wish to follow this up at greater length: Christopher Lamb's *Belief in a Mixed Society* (Lion Publishing, Tring, Herts,1985) studies several questions which make it difficult for people of different faiths to live together, and suggests directions which Christians can take to find a possible way through for everyone; Roger Hooker and John Sergeant (eds) *Belonging to Britain: Christian Perspectives on Religion and Identity in a Plural Society* (CCBI Publications, London, 1991) includes several useful descriptive articles and an important contribution from a Religious Education specialist, Brenda Watson: 'Integrity and Affirmation: an Inclusivist Approach to National Identity', pp.135–148; and my own article 'Together in Birmingham – Strength through Racial Diversity: Religious Plurality in an English City' in *Studies in Interreligious Dialogue*

(Orbis Books, Maryknoll, NY and Kok Pharos, Kampen, Netherlands,1995) vol. 5 no. 2, pp.117–140.

3. *For All God's People – Ecumenical Prayer Cycle* (SPCK with the Catholic Truth Society, London in association with the World Council of Churches, Geneva, and many ot,her publishers in different countries, 1978, p.238); the second edition, 1989, has the title *With all God's People – The New Ecumenical Prayer Cycle* (compiled by John Garden, WCC Publications, Geneva, with an accompanying companion volume of Orders of Service). This cycle seems to have disappeared into the woodwork of the churches, but in one or two cases where I have come across it in regular use, I have been most happily struck by the creativity it releases.

4. The subtitle of William Greider's recent provocative book, *One World Ready or Not* (Simon & Schuster, New York, 1997), which discusses the prospects for the common future of the nations if present economic dogmas continue to rule unchallenged in the government of the USA and among the elites of the World Bank and International Monetary Fund.

5. For those who would like to read more in this field, I warmly recommend, as an example of the kind of thinking now being done in the professional field of Religious Education, Professor John Hull's two articles, 'Christian Education: Sufficient or Necessary?' in *The Epworth Review*, vol. 24 nos 1 and 2, January and April 1997. Not specifically to do with Religious Education, but excellent and forward-looking reading are two recent Occasional Papers from the Selly Oak Colleges (available from the Publications Secretary, Selly Oak Colleges, Birmingham B29 6LQ): *What Will The Third Vatican Council Have to Say about Relations between Christians* and *People of Other Faiths* by Redmond Fitzmaurice OP, and *Yours Inter-Faithfully – An English Christian Tries to Stay Honest* by Christopher Lamb.

6. See, for instance, the *Times Educational Supplement* of 24 October, 1997, reporting on an enlightening study of the differences in attitudes among 14-18 year old Asian girls of different faiths carried out by Dr Harkirtan Singh-Raud of Liverpool John Moores University. The same page also carries a striking article on the difficulties faced by Muslim young women setting out on career paths.

Five

GROWING TOGETHER: THIRTY YEARS ON
John Fitzsimmons

> *Beloved in Christ, can we not make that pilgrimage*
> *together hand in hand?*
> (*Pope John Paul II, Bellahouston Park, Glasgow, 1982*)

The thirty years of the title are from the end of the Second Vatican Council (1962–65) up to the present time. It goes without saying that Vatican II was a 'sea change' in the Roman Catholic Church's attitude to and participation in the ecumenical movement, as it was in so many other things. The period is very conveniently bisected by the papal visit of 1982, and the Pope himself offered a vision:

> *I wish to address for a few moments that larger community of believers in Christ, who share with my Catholic brothers and sisters the privilege of being Scots, sons and daughters alike of this ancient nation . .*
> *We are only pilgrims on this earth, making our way towards the heavenly kingdom promised to us as God's children. Beloved brethren in Christ, for the future, can we not make that pilgrimage together hand-in-hand . . . This would surely bring down upon us the blessing of God our Father on our pilgrim way.*[1]

There is a sense in which this is a real hostage to fortune, because it gives an opportunity to estimate the ecumenical performance of the Roman Catholic Church in Scotland itself, as well as providing some kind of well-intentioned benchmark for other churches.

For the purposes of the present review, the papal remark gives a useful 'dividing-line', because experience shows that there have been, in effect, two phases or stages in the process of growing together – from the early nervous exchanges of the immediate post-conciliar period to the more settled situation of the 1980s and 1990s.

It would, of course, be a mistake to imagine that nothing had happened in this country in terms of the search for Christian unity prior to the 1960s. But it would be true to say that such efforts as there were tended to be sporadic and at the individual and private level (usually as the result of close personal contact between parish ministers, rectors and parish priests in the heavily clericalized style of church life in those days). On the ground, the atmosphere was one of (and this is the most polite word that comes to mind) wariness, if not overt antagonism.[2] There was, and to a certain extent there still is, a kind of Roman Catholic pride and triumphalism which, in spite of public protestations to the contrary, tends to wonder what on earth the Roman Church has to learn from other churches. The assumption was that, given enough time, the other churches would come to their senses and quickly rejoin the house of the common Father, the Bishop of Rome. On the other hand, the churches of the Reform tended to define themselves not so much by what they believed, but rather by marking off those parts of Roman doctrine which they did not believe. There is a residue of both attitudes in this country even today. A kind of tribalism has arisen whereby many who would still define themselves as 'Christians' are much clearer about what they are not than about what they are. There is one further dimension to this which is not often recorded and the present occasion is too good to let it pass. In common with many Roman Catholic scholars, the present writer was astonished by the apparently infallible statements which fell from the lips of our Protestant confrères with regard to Catholic teaching. While we were (of necessity, in the main) in learning mode, we found ourselves confronted with people who thought they knew what the Roman Church taught – often quite erroneously.

One of the documents from that period which perhaps under-lines what has been said is the famous *Agreement and Disagree-*

ment Report of the Church of Scotland.[3] Its origins were curious in that it was originally produced in answer to a request from the Orange Order for the differences between the Roman and Reformed faiths to be spelled out. It is entirely to the credit of the Church of Scotland that the accent was placed on the positive: agreement first, and only then disagreement. It is made clear in the preface that the General Assembly of the Church of Scotland did not necessarily share the premises on which the Grand Orange Lodge of Scotland's petition was based, but had found it useful to remit to the Panel on Doctrine the task of preparing 'a concise statement of the common ground and differences in fundamental belief between the Church of Scotland and the Roman Catholic Church, in order to lead to and ensure a better understanding of both'.[4]

That such a document was possible in 1977 is a testament to the enthusiasm of the first period and also a testament to the Scottish desire to be absolutely sure that agreed texts actually said what they were supposed to say. There had been one or two texts of an ecumenical nature from other parts of the world (especially from south of the border here) which were viewed with suspicion because of what was taken to be 'woolliness' of language. If memory serves well, this was a preoccupation from the very beginning, and yet at the same time many of the Roman Catholic participants had ringing in their ears the words of John XXIII when he opened Vatican II:

> *The substance of the ancient doctrine of the Faith is one thing, and the way in which it is presented is another. And it is the latter that must be taken into great consideration, with patience if necessary, everything being measured in the forms and proportions of a magisterium which is predominantly pastoral in character.*[5]

Looking back, what was happening was that most of us were discovering another theological language; indeed, it was the discovery of another way of 'doing' theology. Even for those of us whose training had been of the highly polished, professional, academic kind in the best schools here and abroad,[6] the ecumenical dialogue was a constant challenge and a real journey of discovery. Methods had to be revised, presuppositions had to be clarified, and above all every stage had to be explained. Some of the early joint reports still show the evidence of 'stitching', i.e. the seams are not invisible and it is possible to do a 'lit. crit.' exercise on most of them, seeing where the contributions of the different traditions have been combined. For people with the biblical, textual and archaeological training of the present writer, such re-readings can be at times fascinating and at times hilarious. On the other hand, it was a necessary stage; later documents tend to place different insights side by side: what can be said together is said, but in many instances there is still as yet a need for a 'synoptic' reading by which comparative study can take place.

At the start, the topics for discussion between the Roman Catholic Church and the other churches tended to concentrate on areas which presented little or no difficulty, or at least so it was thought. The sacrament of baptism seemed a fundamental notion to begin with and it seemed *a priori* that it would present few problems. And yet at one stage there was the completely anomalous situation revealed by the Common Baptismal Certificate of the old British Council of Churches, which listed the Churches that recognized one another's baptisms: that of the Church of Scotland was recognized by the Roman Catholic Church in England and Wales, but not by the Roman Catholic Church in Scotland. The situation was eventually resolved, but it was an early warning to those who imagined that some or any points of contact could be taken for granted.[7] The work done by the Roman and Episcopal Churches in those early days on baptism and the Eucharist has, in the main, stood the test of time,[8] and there is much that can give cause for legitimate pride and satisfaction. However, it is as clear now as it was then that unless the Roman Catholic Church and the Church of Scotland get down to serious business, ecumenism in a Scottish context must remain a sideshow. Due respect must be paid to the work of the Multilateral Church Conversation of those days, but then the Roman Church was merely an observer. The analogy with the position *vis-à-vis* the World Council of Churches should not be lost. The biggest single development towards the end of the 'first period' was a serious engagement between the Church of Scotland and the Roman Catholic Church in this country. It is perhaps entirely in keeping with the whole spirit of relations between these two churches that closer contact began with a significant, practical and (to use a wonderful European ecumenical expression) neuralgic question: the matter of inter-church marriage.

It seems fair to say that the initial discussions on this matter ended in the proverbial 'Mexican Standoff', but out of seeming impasse arose a major step forward, the formation of a Joint Commission on Doctrine. From the beginning, this was an altogether more serious development, because it started with the doctrine of the Church, which for many had been seen as the crucial question in all ecumenical debate.

The work of the Joint Commission on Doctrine did not issue in any great practical revolution; given the nature of its remit and the nature of the topics it covered it would be hard to see how it could. What it did provide, however, was a mature forum for debate between exponents of contemporary Roman Catholicism and Reform theology. The discussions were teethy, hard-edged and sharp – but never abrasive or discourteous. At the end of it all, a series of reports came out which still stand up to close inspection,[9] and above all there was a growing respect for the theological traditions of both churches and a healthy regard for the different ways of 'doing theology' in both traditions. One of the benefits of a variety of backgrounds in the membership of the Joint Commission (on both sides) was an awareness of ecumenical dialogue and its progress outside Scotland. The work of the World Alliance of Reformed Churches and the Groupe des Dombes was taken into account, as was the ongoing work of the (then) Vatican Secretariat for Promoting Christian Unity. The contribution of Faith and Order was taken into account, to say nothing of the Anglican–Roman Catholic International Commission and its work (ARCIC). In this way, there was little danger of the relatively small Scottish body duplicating the excellent work already done or of succumbing to the temptation to reinvent the ecumenical wheel, a temptation which has not entirely been avoided in more recent times. Faith and Order, which of course has strong historical connections with Scotland[10] published its monumental paper no. 111 in the same year as the visit of Pope John Paul. It still stands as one of the major milestones on the 'pilgrim way', especially with regard to the early stages or 'first period' after Vatican II. It carried the simple title *Baptism, Eucharist and Ministry*, and so encapsulated the three main areas where the ecumenical dialogue had been focused up to that point. The more it was discussed, at seminars held to 'tease it out', the more it was promoted within the churches, the more it became apparent that the third element, namely the 'Ministry', was crucial because it laid bare the ecclesiological principles of those who were looking at it. To be more specific: it became more and more clear that there is little point in discussing the pros and cons of various views of the Eucharist if there is no recognition of the ministry that celebrates that Eucharist. In turn, however, there is no clear way of finding agreement with regard to the idea of ministry unless there is some understanding of ministry itself and also of the Church that confers that ministry. In this way, the *BEM* document of Faith and Order acted as something of a catalyst and came as a welcome stimulus to those who for long and weary years had been suggesting that the theology of the Church lay at the heart of the ecumenical project. It is a fact that for most people the Church is the primary datum; their understanding of the gospel and ultimately of Christ himself is derived from the Church to which they belong. Over the centuries this Church has become denominationalized: East and West, Roman and non-Roman, hierarchical and non-hierarchical, sacramental and non-sacramental . . . Faith and Order hints at this.[11] The discussion, inevitably, pushes the churches backwards to the New Testament itself and therein lies not so much the safe haven in which all will find rest, but rather another battlefield which will in due course lay bare just how deep the divisions among the churches have become.

Three stages on the journey

By the end of the 'first period', three things had become apparent.

– Firstly, in these islands people had been singularly unprepared for the blossoming of the ecumenical spirit after Vatican II. This is especially true of the Roman Catholic community itself; but if there is a strength in the Roman system it is this – the voice of authority is still heeded. So when the Council spoke, the Church listened. Pope John XXIII's idea of 'opening the windows' or providing the Church with an updating (*aggiornamento*) was invested with all of the weight of his predecessors. Even his bitterest enemies (of whom there were many immediately around the papal throne) recognized that the old dictum, '*Roma locuta est, causa finita est*', was still in vigour. What they then set about doing was to deprive the Council of its impact, and this is what is going on today.[12] And so it was that many Roman Catholics, in a spirit of complete loyalty to the Holy See (as they saw it), tried to come to terms with an ecclesial 'brave new world' that was for them a call to launch into the deep such as most had never expected to be confronted with in their lifetime. Doubtless the same is true of many members of other churches, but it is only fair to record the 'sensus fidelium' of ordinary Catholic people which led them, in spite of themselves, to engage in closer contact with Christians of other traditions. There are many happy recollections of services during the Octave of Prayer for Christian Unity which were filled with enthusiasm and a genuine sharing of the Spirit. There are also, of course, memories which make the flesh creep, born as they were out of utterances made in pure ignorance of other people's faith and practice. It was all part of a learning process; all the churches were on what is now called a 'learning curve', and for many a Roman Catholic that was a revelation in itself. Just as the people in the pews showed such a taste for ecumenical contact, it remains a hope for the future that their 'sense' will guide the churches into the other phases of contact and mutual understanding.

– Secondly, there had been a certain clearing of the air. Theological debate was being carried out at a higher, more intense and less polite level. The real issues were beginning to dominate the agenda: the rationale for separate Catholic schools, the Roman Church's legislation on mixed and inter-church marriages, the thorny question of intercommunion, the divergences between the church of Rome and the other churches on moral matters (abortion, primarily) had all been placed firmly within a theological context which represented sparse and painfully-gained – but solid – results for a lot of effort on the part of a whole host of people.

Above all, there was a certain air of confidence in coming together; not only had personal friendships been made, but professional respect had grown and a common theological language was on the way to being forged. In retrospect, it seems clear enough that what had actually taken place was what the French in their wisdom refer to as 'la purification des mémoires'. In plain English, this really means 'getting it out of your system'. This is no reflection on anyone's 'system'; it is simply a reflection on the attrition of so many years of separation. By the time the Pope visited Scotland, the setting was right; the applause that greeted his remark in Bellahouston Park was genuine, because it reflected where the Roman Catholic community was 'at', and seemed to hold so much promise for the future.

– Thirdly, it is hard to overestimate the contribution of what has become known as 'liturgical convergence'. United services and discussion of the sacraments had led to the point where there was serious discussion of the worship traditions of the churches. This just happened to coincide with the greatest renewal of the Roman liturgy since the days of Gregory the Great and Gelasius.[13] In essence, what took place was the rediscovery of the word of God and its place within the public worship of the Church by Roman Catholics and the parallel rediscovery of the importance of the sacraments by other churches. The balance of 'word and sacrament' was well on its way to being established as the norm, not the exception. The issuing in 1969 of the first edition of the Roman *Ordo Lectionum Missae* took the Christian world by storm, to the extent that many of the churches which had been in the process of revising their presentation of the word were captivated by it.[14] Its potential was quickly perceived and the Consultation on Common Texts (CCT) in North America got to work on it and in due course produced the *Common Lectionary*.[15] At the same time, many of the churches had gone back to the sources and rediscovered the riches of the *Anaphora* of Hippolytus and the great sacramentaries, thereby following the same path as the Roman Church had trodden in producing the Missal of Paul VI in 1969. All at once the principle 'Lex Orandi, Lex Credendi' took on a further significance – one that was destined to assume greater importance as time went on. Even a brief examination of the liturgy in use at the World Council of Churches' gathering in Vancouver in 1983 is enough to make the point: the 'liturgical convergence' is mighty and nudges the churches towards the future.

New ecumenical instruments

The years following the papal visit to Britain are dominated in ecumenical terms by the development of new 'instruments'. The actual detail of the process is spelled out in what became known as the 'Marigold Book' – a somewhat soft name for a quite hard-headed document.[16] The section on Scotland, pp.49–59, is the basic outline of ACTS and its work.

> *The general purpose of 'Action of Churches Together in Scotland' continues the general purpose of Scottish Churches' Council, namely 'to further the mission and realize the unity of the Church universal by providing a national focus of Inter-Church counsel and action.'*
> (p.49)

While on the face of it this is wholly unexceptionable, it also points up the weakness in the Scottish ecumenical scene: as yet there is precious little sense of the 'Church Universal' in all the activity of the churches in this land. There is still far too much care given to national and indeed local issues and concerns. One

For God's Sake ... Unity

of the major concerns at the time of the formation of the new
ecumenical instruments was that they would simply turn into
other ways of continuing to do what had been done already. Indeed, it went deeper than that; there were many people who
were afraid that their formation would provide the churches
with a perfect excuse for going over old ground and reinventing
the ecumenical wheel. It depends to a large extent on how fresh
people are to the whole business whether or not this impression
or fear is reinforced. In the case of the present writer, the reaction must be that 'the jury is still out', since there is an abiding
impression that hierarchs (of all churches, not simply the Roman Church) are happy to be seen engaging in earnest ecumenical
dialogue – and being 'nice' to one another – providing there are
no hard and fast changes to be made and no threats to vested
interests.[17]

It is noticeable, although not entirely surprising, how much of
the Marigold Book's treatment of ACTS and its activity is taken
up with structures and finance. The casual observer might be forgiven for mistaking it for the prospectus of a variety of com-
panies presenting themselves for merger, if not exactly for
take-over. The inspiration, however, is sound and is well expressed in the conclusion to the section on Scotland:

> We believe that the above proposals are true to the vis-
> ion of the Inter-Church Process, are flexible and provi-
> sional, and can be an effective means by which the
> Scottish Churches may give substance to their commit-
> ment to one another and their common commitment
> to the one God, Father, Son, and Holy Spirit. (p.59)

The order is interesting: commitment to one another and then
to the Trinity; at least one reading of history suggests that that
has always been the problem with the Church – putting itself
first and then (only then) speaking of God. The essential spirit
of the new instrument, however, is something from which no
one in their right senses could possibly differ: 'Churches Together in Pilgrimage' – an echo, perhaps conscious, of Pope John
Paul's Glasgow invitation. The celebration of the inauguration of

108

the new Council of Churches of Britain and Ireland (CCBI) was memorable for a variety of reasons. Abiding memories are of walking along Hope Street in Liverpool, from the Anglican cathedral to the Roman Catholic Metropolitan cathedral, in the company of John Smith, by common consent one of the best Prime Ministers this country never had. The talk was of hope: hope not only for advancing Christian unity, but of what a united and uniting Church could do for the great underclass in these islands (then groaning under the weight of Thatcherism at its height); the language of 'social exclusion' had not quite been developed at that time. If ever there was a time when the biblical, Judaeo-Christian model of 'Let My People Go' seemed appropriate, it was then. There were anomalies too – not least in the affinity that seemed to be found between the most dogmatic of churches (the Roman in particular) and the most 'relaxed' (such as some of the Afro-West Indian churches).[18] After that, it was time for the churches to settle down and make the instruments work – though there is still the vivid recollection of reporting back on behalf of a discussion group (made up of delegates mainly from Scotland, Wales and Northern Ireland) that the time was short and the New Deal was on trial; what effect this had on Basil Hume and John Habgood was hard to tell.[19]

In Scotland, ACTS got to work and the first thing that has to be recorded is the joy experienced by those who had been at the 'coal face' for some time in meeting new friends and gaining a sense of common strength and bonding for the future. The many commissions and committees of ACTS can answer for themselves; the experience of those who made up and presently make up the Commission on Unity, Faith and Order (UFO) has been mixed.[20] There was initially a tendency to retread old ground and that was a trial and source of frustration to many; there was also a period of harking back to a former age when people seemed to think they were being threatened or that their most cherished beliefs and practices were 'up for grabs'. There was also a sense of *déjà vu* in that documents of a bygone era were being recycled and old battles (which had either been won or lost) re-fought. It is entirely to the credit of the convener and the secretary that the commission was able to move on at all. The catalyst in its work came from the suggestion that there might be, in the year 2001, a 'General Assembly of the Churches in Scotland'. After a degree of initial misunderstanding,[21] the commission appointed a 'working party' (normally a sentence of death in ecumenical circles, almost as bad as being 'commended to the churches for study and comment') and it has done its work well, to the point where the churches have been forced to take some kind of principled stand. From the very outset, it was clear that another 'talking shop' was not needed; the spirit of the age demanded something better and more adventurous. Such an 'assembly', it was quickly noted, could only carry interest and weight if it were composed of people who could genuinely speak on behalf of their respective churches and vote on matters of common 'policy'. This is not the same as reinventing the councils of the first four centuries, nor is it the recipe for some kind of 'lowest common denominator' Christianity that all can call their own. Rather, it is a gathering of Christians of every tradition who can confront issues of common concern not only to the churches in this country but to the people of this country at large and who can give a united and cogent response to those issues in the light of an agreed understanding of the gospel. Such an idea poses a challenge to Roman sensibilities, where the temptation is always to imagine that the Holy See has already dealt with these things and the answers lie in papal documents of one kind or another; and to Protestant churches whose awareness of the practical issues of ordinary life at the tail end of the twentieth century sometimes leaves a lot to be desired, given that many of them have abandoned any attempt to provide clear and authoritative moral guidance. The problem with Rome, as many see it (including many who see it from within), is that it seems to be handing out certainties where they do not exist; the problem with the others is that they do not seem to have any certainties at all.

The Cardinal Archbishop of Glasgow seemed to endorse the notion of the Assembly of Churches when he addressed the

General Assembly of the Church of Scotland. Whether His Eminence had thought through the implications of such an endorsement is another matter; certainly there is no immediate recollection of consultation between him or his press office or advisers with the Working Party or the Commission of ACTS. It would be a pity if such a good idea were to founder because the sponsoring churches took 'cold feet' at the last moment. [22]

Papal encyclical: 'Ut Unum Sint'

In the 1990s there have been two major contributions to the ecumenical scene emanating from Rome: the Ecumenical Directory of 25 March, 1993 and the Encyclical Letter of Pope John Paul II 'Ut Unum Sint', of 25 May, 1995.[23] Reaction to the first was initially enthusiastic – that is, until scholars and others had had time to study it at closer quarters. The more mature reaction could be summed up in this way: a sense of wonder as to where the composers of the Directory had been in the years since Vatican II. It seems to look forward to things which are already in place; it seems to speak of things as 'desirable' when in fact they have been recognized as 'essential'. The section on liturgical convergence is frankly derisory and gives the impression that the Roman dicastery concerned with ecumenism had in no wise been in consultation with the corresponding dicastery concerned with liturgical matters, or perhaps had received bad advice from the Congregation for Divine Worship.[24] Like many another recent Roman document, the Directory is good on general principles and statements of ideals, and very much at home when dealing with the internal structures of the Roman Church. The section on the sacraments is a very mixed bag, and it is no great surprise that the text concerning the admission of members of other churches and 'ecclesial communities' to the Eucharist was variously interpreted as restrictive and as opening a small chink in the otherwise impenetrable armour of the Roman Church on the subject. Now that the dust has settled, it is clear that those who took the former view were in the right. Somewhat disappointingly, the appeal for authority in the Directory is made not to the gospel or to the experience of those already engaged in ecumenical dialogue, but rather to the Code of Canon Law and to a whole host of the Holy See's previous utterances. Those who had seen the Directory in some of its earlier draft versions were well aware that the final text bore all the hallmarks of the severe editorial style of the Congregation for the Doctrine of the Faith presided over by Cardinal Joseph Ratzinger.[25] It is all the more pleasant, therefore, to remark that the content and tone of the papal encyclical letter 'Ut Unum Sint' is entirely different. Here there is genuine contact with the gospel; here there is sincerity and humility of tone; here there is a frank acknowledgement that the papacy and its exercise has, historically, been an obstacle to the reunification of the Church, a hindrance to many – not a help. Here there is also an open invitation to the other churches to engage in frank no-holds-barred discussion of the 'Petrine Ministry' against the background of the papal claim (which is once again explicitly made) to universal and supreme jurisdiction over the entire Church. The final chapter is entitled 'Quanta Est Nobis Via?' – i.e. 'How far do we still have to go?' On the evidence of the letter itself, the answer must be 'a long way'. The show is given away on pages 107–8: the communion of particular churches with the Church of Rome is a necessary condition for unity. Indeed, the text goes further: such a condition for unity is 'in God's plan'.[26] There were, initially, some very peculiar reactions to the encyclical – not least on the part of some reactionary Roman prelates who stoutly maintained that there was no room for comment from Roman Catholic scholars and others; the discussion was for the other churches, it was said, because no Roman Catholic would wish to differ from the papal text.[27] Once a modicum of common sense had prevailed, there was the further difficulty that many Roman Catholic participants in the forming of 'responses' to the document either felt unable to be identified or were excluded from subscribing to such responses. The Commission of ACTS was baffled by this particular piece of 'double-think' and continues to be baffled. Roman Catholic reflection and theological debate on the Petrine ministry is no more uni-vocal and monolithic than it is on many another matter. At least those who took part in the Consultation organized on Iona by the Iona Community felt no such scruples and their response is all the better for it in breadth and honesty. It may be too early yet to estimate the impact of the Pope's letter; it looks at the moment, however, to be a 'diamond in a coal mine', a rare outbreak of honesty and 'cards on the table'. In this sense, it is a genuine challenge, because it does what the Roman Church is good at doing – putting down a marker to which others can either draw near or by which they will feel repelled. It is a virtue of the Roman system that such 'markers' are possible; it is not at all possible for some other churches and (at best) very difficult for yet others. It may be polite to suggest that 'the jury is out'; on the other hand, there is always the suspicion that that is precisely how church leaders like it.

Three issues

To take the cue from the Pope's letter: Quanta Est Nobis Via? There are several areas which are crying out for serious consideration in the ecumenical dialogue in this nation.

– Firstly, at a time when the national consciousness has been identified and reinforced (in the referendum debate/vote and the establishment of a Scottish parliament), the churches must get their act together to make sure that there is proper input to the counsels of the nation. If there is one thing that has been learned over the past thirty years (whether in the first period or the second), it is this: the world at large refuses to take the churches seriously when they speak with a divided voice. There is one fundamental ecumenical principle which is often forgotten and which becomes more important with each passing day – never do separately what can be done together. The issues facing the majority of our people are issues which transcend denominationalism: poverty – or 'social exclusion', which comes to the same thing – employment or lack of it, the care of the elderly, the sick,

and the children (including, of course, the unborn), and the great
focal point, namely 'education, education, education'. If there
was ever anything destined to resonate with the Scots it is surely
this last. Perhaps the foreseen Assembly of Churches in 2001 will
be able to address these and formulate common 'policy' for the
churches to deal with them and address the Scottish parliament
with a united voice. Perhaps it will help the nation to raise its
head to look beyond its own borders and see the deprivation and
want in other lands; maybe it will be able to raise the level of consciousness here about the effects of our greed on less resourced
areas of the world. The point is this, however: the voice of the
churches must be the voice of Christ – not raised in condemna-
tion, but in regret and hope for the future. The year 1998 has
been designated the 'Year of Hope' by those who are keen on the
Millennium, the present Pope included. It is to be hoped that the
churches in this country will find their common voice, not only
with regard to writing off Third World debt, but also with regard
to the issues which daily confront their own people.

– Secondly, someone somewhere has to loosen up the log-jam
of intercommunion. The exceptions which are present in the
Roman discipline successfully demonstrate that the Eucharist
can be separated from the doctrine of the visible unity of the
Church – when it is necessary 'for pastoral reasons' or in other
circumstances of acute need. There is room for development
here: an expansion of the 'exceptions' carried out 'for ecumenical
reasons' might indicate that there are more exceptions than
rules. On the other hand, the various other churches will have to
come clean with regard to their faith in the Real Presence. There
is not nor could there be any requirement to accept the doctrine
of transubstantiation (a doctrine which is but rarely found in its
pure form, even among Catholics today); but there must be a
measure of agreement as to what we think we are doing together
at the Eucharist. The traditional Roman view is that of the
'higher' eucharistic theology, in which the Eucharist is the summit towards which the search for Christian unity is tending.
There is, however, another way: the Eucharist can also be

thought of as the source from which the search for Christian unity draws its strength and direction. The Vatican II image of 'culmen et fons'[28] can provide a useful model in this whole question. One thing is certain – something must be done quickly if the situation is not to degenerate into a free-for-all and good and committed people lose heart for want of encouragement.

– Thirdly, the doctrine of the Church itself has to be addressed seriously. The text of the first World Conference on Faith and Order at Lausanne in 1927 (referred to by *BEM* in note 26 and the commentary thereon) reads in part:

> *In view of the place which the episcopate, the council of presbyters, and the congregation of the faithful respectively, had in the constitution of the early Church, and the fact that episcopal, presbyteral and congregational systems of government are each today, and have been for centuries, accepted by great communions in Christendom, and the fact that episcopal, presbyteral and congregational are each believed by many to be essential to the good order of the Church, we therefore recognize that these several elements must all, under conditions which require further study, have an appropriate place in the order of life of a reunited Church.*[29]

Some will find elements of this contentious, but it is their very contentiousness which makes them matters of urgency. The underlying question is this: are there elements in any of the churches which can be identified as there by the will of God? Are there elements in some churches which are absent from others and which render those churches either imperfect or even not 'churches' at all? These questions have indeed been raised before, but the time has come to confront them head-on and stop circling warily round the edges. Great encouragement can be taken from recent expressions of commitment to hard-edged dialogue that will produce lasting results for the longer-term future.

NOTES

1. See *The Pope in Britain: Collected Homilies and Speeches* (texts issued by the Vatican Press Office and released by the Catholic Information Services, Slough, 1982). It should be noted that the end of the passage is followed by the conventional sign for (sustained) applause. If memory serves, the Pope's homily that day was interrupted many times but at this point with particular enthusiasm.

2. As a native of Paisley, the present writer can well recall what happened when the minister of Paisley Abbey, Doctor Rogan, sought help from the wider community in preserving this 'jewel'. The redoubtable Monsignor Frederick Raphael Pirrie (himself a convert to Catholicism) commended the appeal on the grounds that 'we should like it in the best possible condition when it is restored to its rightful owners'. That was in the fifties, and both Rogan and Pirrie were (in retrospect) more enlightened than most of their contemporaries.

3. *Agreement and Disagreement: The Common Ground and Major Differences in Belief between the Church of Scotland and the Roman Catholic Church* (2nd edition, revised and edited by Alasdair I. C. Heron, Edinburgh 1984). In the editor's foreword there is reference to 'the good offices of a Roman Catholic colleague, who wishes to remain anonymous, for taking the time and trouble to list comprehensively his suggestions for improvement, many (if not all!) of which have been incorporated'. The Roman Catholic colleague in question was the present writer and there is nothing sinister in the anonymity: it was simply to get the points made without having to go through the machinery of committees, commissions and the like. The work was actually done in Rome, where both of us were attending a meeting involving the Holy See and the World Alliance of Reformed Churches.

4. Op. cit. 'Preface to the First Edition', p.7.

5. See *The Documents of Vatican II: With Notes and Comments by Catholic, Protestant and Orthodox Authorities* (Walter M. Abbott and Joseph Gallagher (eds.), London and Dublin, 1966) p.715.

6. In the case of the present writer, the Pontifical Gregorian University, Rome (Ph.L.,, 1959; STL, 1963); the Pontifical Biblical Institute, Rome and Jerusalem (LSS, 1965); The École Biblique, Jerusalem; the Hebrew University, Jerusalem. In all candour, there was a form of 'culture shock' on returning to Scotland. While my Roman and other mentors had been careful to introduce me to the best of Protestant and other non-Catholic scholarship, my peers in this country were singularly insular in their awareness – with the exception of a few Bultmannians and more numerous neo-Barthians, continental scholarship was not on the menu. Roman Catholic scholarship might as well not have existed. Happily all of that has changed. If anything, it is the present-day Roman exponents who demonstrate insularity. As a colleague, well-versed in the ways of Rome, used to say, 'Triumphalism is not dead – it is merely forbidden.'

7. The matter of mutual recognition of baptism was a matter of personal con-

cern. Although brought up a Presbyterian, my mother had been baptized in the Scottish Episcopal Church. On becoming a Roman Catholic she was (I think conditionally) re-baptized. This had always rankled – with her and with me. I was glad to have had a part to play in sorting out the scandal of non-recognition. As it seems now, the argument was essentially anecdotal: the vagaries of individual ministers were confused with the practice of their churches.

8. See *The Nature of Baptism and Its Place in the Life of the Church* (Glasgow, 1969); *The Ecclesial Nature of the Eucharist* (Glasgow, 1973). Both these documents are described as 'Reports' from the 'Joint Study Group of Representatives of the Roman Catholic Church in Scotland and the Scottish Episcopal Church'. Both were approved by the bishops of the respective churches. The use of the term 'representatives' is interesting, because there did not seem to be the same reticence then (as there is now) about the representative capacity of delegates from churches. The nebulous nature of the capacity in which people presently speak at ecumenical gatherings is one of the key issues that must be sorted out if there is to be genuine progress. It is also characteristic of the cautiousness of the 'second period'.

9. The essence of the argument from both sides on the question of the nature of the Church can be found in the document *Towards a Common Understanding of the Church. Reformed/Roman Catholic International Dialogue : Second Phase, 1984–1990* (Geneva: World Alliance of Reformed Churches, 1991, pp.34–40). Those involved in producing this report included Revd Prof. Dr Alasdair I. C. Heron (Erlangen), Revd Dr Alan S. Lewis (Edinburgh) and the present writer.

10. It seems clear that the Faith and Order movement was a prime mover in the development of the twentieth-century ecumenical movement itself, between the Edinburgh Conference of 1910 and the formation of the World Council of Churches in 1948. It is commonly regarded as providing the most representative theological forum in the world.

11. See *Baptism Eucharist and Ministry: Faith and Order Paper no 111* (World Council of Churches, Geneva, 1982) no. 26, pp.25–26, plus commentary on p.26. The reference to the World Conference at Lausanne in 1927 is especially worthy of note.

12. It is too early to estimate the pontificate of John XXIII; what is said about his 'enemies' here goes back to personal reminiscence, but is also confirmed by Peter Hebblethwaite in *John XXIII, Pope of the Council* (London, 1984) and in the sequel *Paul VI: The First Modern Pope* (London, 1993).

13. The Mass formularies of Gelasius were preserved in the Leonine Sacramentary (sixth century) and the influence of Gregory on the Roman Mass is still to be seen today. It is a great mystery to the present writer that there are still those who would wish to go back to 'the Latin Mass' when what they really mean is the awful 'hotch-potch' of 14 July, 1570. The so-called Mass of Paul VI is without doubt a compromise – but it is better than its predecessor. See J. N. D. Kelly, *The Oxford Dictionary of Popes* (Oxford, 1986)

and Richard P. McBrien, *Lives of the Popes* (San Francisco, 1997).

14. *Ordo Lectionum Missae* (Vatican Press, 1969) is merely a set of biblical references; it has since been rendered in a three-volume edition with the readings in place. The North American Consultation on Common Texts first produced *The Common Lectionary* (New York, 1983) on the basis of work that had been going on since the late 1970s. In the light of study and comment, it then issued *The Revised Common Lectionary* (Norwich, 1992). Since that time it has commended itself to churches in other linguistic areas: German, French and (above all) Spanish.

15. 'The Revised Common Lectionary and its earlier edition of 1983 continue the pattern of the Roman Lectionary for Mass 1969 . . . The Revised Common Lectionary accepts the *cornerstone* of the Roman Lectionary . . . The Revised Common Lectionary along with its Roman parent . . .' See *The Revised Common Lectionary* (Norwich, 1992), pp. 12–13. The present writer was part of the 'Task Force' which put the whole thing together in the spirit of the Roman OLM.

16. *Churches Together in Pilgrimage: Including Definitive Proposals for Ecumenical Instruments* (London, 1989). In a sense, the document is too 'hard-headed', in that much is said about structures, procedures and finances and the spirit of the movement behind it tends to be somewhat obscured.

17. It is, of course, entirely for the good that the 'leaders' of various churches should meet and offer one another hospitality. The tendency has been, however, to allow this to pass for ecumenism: it is important to be seen to be engaged in dialogue – it is noticeable that when the dialogue becomes a serious matter and 'too close to the bone', ranks are closed.

18. The greatest anomaly, if not humiliation, was witnessing the Roman Catholic Church in Ireland reduced to the level of 'observer' and taking its place with such as the 'Countess of Huntingdon's Connexion'. Thankfully, this has since been rectified.

19. In retrospect, the placing of the 'leaders' on the top step was a mistake: they were an easy target for frustration and they made the whole thing look like an ecclesiastical exercise in public relations – what the Italians call a 'montatura'.

20. There was a good deal of floundering to begin with, and the commission was within an ace of succumbing to the temptation to reinvent the ecumenical wheel. However, quite soon the perennial topics of intercommunion and inter-church marriage concentrated its mind wonderfully.

21. Starting from the perception that many still saw the General Assembly of the Church of Scotland as the nearest thing this country had (at that time) to a Parliament and that the Kirk spoke for the nation, the suggestion was made that such an idea should be 'deconstructed'. This was interpreted as a call for the deconstruction of the Kirk – a task well beyond the remit of the commission and, in the opinion of some at least, a task almost beyond the strength of the Holy Spirit.

22. There is, and for many years has been, a degree of restlessness in the churches with leaders who make grand and hopeful statements which are never fol-

lowed up. It is a question whether the cardinal realized what he was getting into with his remarks. There has developed a style in church affairs as in politics of being long on rhetoric and short on 'follow-through'. It is to be hoped that this is not another example.

23. Pontificium Consilium ad Christianorum Unitatem Fovendam. *Directory for the Application of Principles and Norms on Ecumenism* (London, 1993); *Encyclical Letter, Ut Unum Sint, of the Holy Father John Paul II on Commitment to Ecumenism* (Vatican City, 1995). Years of protest to Vatican officials about the quality of English used in their documents have yielded nothing; in both of these, there is not even a good level of 'eurospeak' – rather, it is the usual 'oblique vaticanese' which is on display.

24. Ten years as a consultor to the Congregation for Divine Worship and the Discipline of the Sacraments would lead to the conclusion that the latter is probably the case. This dicastery does not feature high up in the Vatican 'pecking order'. It is under-funded, under-resourced, and above all lacks competent personnel. The Pontifical Council for Promoting Christian Unity, on the other hand, has an abundance of competent personnel but is similarly under-funded and under-resourced.

25. Anyone familiar with the work of the Roman Curia would know that *everything* has to go through Ratzinger's office. It is worth recalling to non-Romans that the previous title of his department was 'The Holy Office', which was short for 'The Holy Office of Inquisition'. The last Peter Hebblethwaite book, *The New Inquisition?* (London, 1980), posed the question. The answer is pending.

26. The edition to hand is that of the Vatican Press; the relevant texts are to be found in section 97.

27. The strictures of John Cardinal O'Connor on his episcopal brother John Raphael Quinn of San Francisco were particularly bizarre and gratuitous.

28. See 'Sacrosanctum Concilium', Constitution on the Sacred Liturgy of Vatican II (4/12/63), no. 10; ET: 'The Liturgy is the summit towards which the activity of the Church is directed; at the same time it is the fountain from which all her power flows.' (Abbott–Gallagher, p.142).

29. *BEM*, no. 26, pp.25–26 and commentary, p.26.

Six

THINK GLOBAL – ACT LOCAL
Murdoch MacKenzie

> *Love the Lord your God with all your heart, with all your soul, and with all your strength, and with all your mind; and your neighbour as yourself.*
> *(Luke 10.27)*

By George

Here is a Christmas card which I received on 11 December, 1989 from George MacLeod, the founder of the Iona Community:

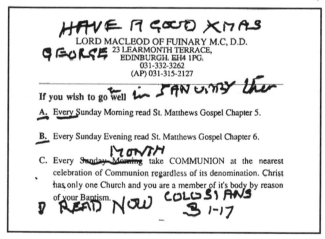

Colossians 3 paints a global picture of a cosmic Christ in whose world there cannot be Greek and Jew, circumcised and uncircumcised, barbarian, Scythian, slave and free man. It gives the wide ecumenical vision of Christ as all and in all. Matthew 5 and 6, the Sermon on the Mount, applies that vision to particular local situations and circumstances such as going a second mile, loving your enemy and not being anxious about tomorrow.

For George MacLeod, the global had to be rooted in the local and this rooting found its focus in communion at the nearest church. The fullness of the universal Church is manifested in the local eucharistic community.[1]

- The wide ecumenical vision of the *oikoumene* as the household of the world finds its touchstone in the nearest church. As Lesslie Newbigin emphasizes in his book *The Gospel in a Pluralist Society*, the local congregation is the hermeneutic of the Gospel.[2]

- Similarly, for George MacLeod the work of the Iona Community was not what happened on Iona, nor what happened in plenary meetings of members, but what was happening in the local areas where community members were living. In other words, there was no point in coming to Iona to make idealistic affirmations about loving God, if you could not love your neighbour back at the ranch. It is sometimes easier to experience the ecumenical vision at an ecumenical assembly, such as that at Graz, than it is walking down the local High Street and seeing the five churches of five different denominations strung out in a line. At such moments, the challenge of George MacLeod's Christmas card becomes acute and his vision of a day when a Roman Catholic priest would celebrate Mass in Iona Abbey, to which everyone would be invited, seems depressingly distant.

Top down or bottom up?

Not forgetting that in a very real sense the first ecumenical movement in Britain came with the formation of the Evangelical Alliance by John Angell James and others in the middle of the nineteenth century, it is normal to look to Edinburgh 1910 as the springboard for Christian unity. A useful summary of the many assemblies, conferences and international gatherings held since then up to 1993 is presented in the booklet *The Ecumenical Scene – A Brief History of Ecumenical Relations in the Past Hundred Years* by Jill Evans.[3]

Up until the early 1960s, much of this ecumenical work was heavily criticized for being imposed from above. Well-meaning people met, not exactly in smoke-filled rooms, although they often were, and suggested grandiose schemes which were not acceptable at local level. Some schemes did come to fruition, as in the Church of Scotland in 1929 and in the Methodist Church in 1932. But, with the notable exception of the Church of South India in 1947, it seemed impossible to hope for any real visible unity between those churches which saw *episcope* as personal and those which saw it as communal.

However, such movements as the Women's World Day of Prayer, founded in America in 1890, and the Week of Prayer for Christian Unity, begun in 1935 by Abbé Paul Couturier, as well as hopes for future Anglican–Methodist unity, encouraged local Christians to work more closely together. This was particularly true in new housing areas in England. The main development in Scotland came in 1963 with a resolution of the Scottish Faith and Order Conference to explore such possibilities in Livingston New Town. By 1966 the Church of Scotland, the Scottish Episcopal Church and the Congregational Union of Scotland had agreed to designate the New Town of Livingston 'an area of ecumenical experiment'.

Meanwhile in England, at the Nottingham Conference on Faith and Order in 1964, the churches were called to

> designate areas of ecumenical experiment, at the request of local congregations, or in new towns and housing areas. In such areas there should be experiments in ecumenical group ministries, in the sharing of buildings and equipment, and in the development of mission.[4]

In 1969 the Sharing of Church Buildings Act was passed by Parliament, which quite literally unlocked the door for a grassroots ecumenical movement to begin from the bottom up. Originally such local experiments were known as Local Ecumenical Projects (LEPs), but recently this has been changed to Local Ecumenical Partnerships. There are now 800 of these in

England and approximate figures by denomination for 1992 are as follows: [5]

1. United Reformed Church	396 LEPs	23% of all its churches
2. Baptist Union	165 LEPs	10% of all its churches
3. Methodist Church	579 LEPs	8% of all its churches
4. Roman Catholic Church	174 LEPs	6% of all its churches
5. Church of England	373 LEPs	2% of all its churches

The acknowledgement of an Area of Local Ecumenical Experiment enabled local people to put their ecumenical vision into practice and cut through such Gordian knots as infant and adult baptism, personal or communal *episcope*, alcoholic or non-alcoholic wine, mutual recognition of ministry and joint confirmation. It was now possible to go to your nearest church and to work and worship together with Christians of all denominations from your own locality. Initiatives could now be taken at the grassroots without waiting for agreements and permission to trickle down from above.

Travelling together

Whilst there are something approaching one hundred Ecumenical Partnerships in Wales and some twenty in Scotland, it is particularly in England that they have blossomed. The accompanying literature about them has also blossomed, as reference to the notes at the end of this chapter will bear witness. Of particular interest is *Travelling Together* by Elizabeth Welch and Flora Winfield, which is a handbook on Local Ecumenical Partnerships. In the foreword Hugh Cross, former Moderator of Churches Together in England Forum, writes:

> *The frequent use of the word 'ecumenism' gives the impression that we are dealing with something static and incapable of change. The truth is that we are being caught up more and more into the ecumenical movement. We are pilgrims on a journey to a distant goal, passing through landscape which changes as we travel*

together. It is not only the landscape which is changing, but ourselves, although we do not always see the changes until some time after they have taken place.

LEPs have changed over the years. They were tentative at the beginning and a bit precious, but as the years have passed and their confidence has grown with their numbers, so they have come to make a number of significant changes to the life of the churches which sponsored them. Far from being the tender plants of yesterday, they continue to demonstrate that they are the foretaste of what is to come, the first fruits of that unity for which we all seek.[6]

With the failure of the English Covenant proposals in the early 1980s, it looked as though all the local initiatives in LEPs were stranded on a sandbank from which the tide was moving out, never to return. But soon an incoming tide was experienced as people fastened on to the words of Pope John Paul II who, on his visit to Britain, suggested that we were strangers no longer, but pilgrims together and that we should walk hand in hand. In response to this, people from Britain and Ireland came to a historic ecumenical gathering at the Hayes Conference Centre, Swanwick, in September 1987. Their joint experience of the Holy Spirit was articulated in the Swanwick Declaration made on 4 September:

We affirm our openness to this growing unity in obedience to the Word of God, so that we may fully share, hold in common and offer to the world those gifts which we have received and still hold in separation. In the unity we seek we recognize that there will not be uniformity, but legitimate diversity . . . It is our conviction that, as a matter of policy at all levels and in all places, our Churches must now move from co-operation to clear commitment to each other, in search of the unity for which Christ prayed and in common evangelism and service of the world.

By the autumn of 1990 the British Council of Churches was

replaced by CTE – Churches Together in England; ACTS – Action of Churches Together in Scotland; CYTUN – Churches Together in Wales. The relationship with Ireland was maintained through the Irish Council of Churches, and the Council of Churches for Britain and Ireland provided a meeting place for all of these. As far as Churches Together in England was concerned, two of its aims were:

> *To promote, co-ordinate, support and service intermediate bodies in England, assisting them in their care for local ecumenical activity and representing their concerns at the national level.*
>
> *To promote the appointment and support of full- or part-time ecumenical officers or their equivalents at the intermediate level throughout England.*

As a result of all this, local ecumenical initiatives were no longer left beached on a sandbank, but were suddenly refloated on a great wave of ecumenical activity which still continues. There are now approximately fifty intermediate ecumenical bodies operating at county level, most of which have a part-time, if not full-time, ecumenical officer whose work includes the promotion and servicing of local ecumenical initiatives. The best description of this work is given in *This Growing Unity* by Roger Nunn.[7]

In all four nations of England, Ireland, Scotland and Wales there has been a serious attempt to practise the Lund dictum of doing things together, except those things which still need to be done separately. The following Pilgrim Prayer, taken from the Swanwick Declaration, is now in general use:

> *Lord God, we thank you*
> *For calling us into the company*
> *Of those who trust in Christ*
> *And seek to obey his will.*
> *May your Spirit guide and strengthen us*
> *In mission and service to your world;*

For we are strangers no longer,
But pilgrims together on the way to your Kingdom.
Amen.

As far as England is concerned, the working out of the Lund principle is enshrined in the *Suggested Rules of Good Practice* which help to keep people, at all levels of church life, thinking ecumenically. At the same time a whole series of other measures has been put in place which enable local people to work and worship together. These include model Covenants and Sharing Agreements, Canons B43 and B44 of the Church of England (equivalent to some of the enabling legislation enacted by the Church of Scotland with respect to Livingston Ecumenical Parish), agreements on baptismal policy between Baptists and other churches and the very extensive work done over many years by the Methodist and United Reformed Churches, including Model Constitutional Guidelines for a joint Methodist and United Reformed Church. Of particular importance has been the development of joint Services of Confirmation in which Anglican bishops share with Free Church ministers in confirming candidates into each of their churches. In addition to the Sharing of Church Buildings Act of 1969, all of the above measures have enabled local people *to share together in their nearest church.*

As illustrations of how such sharing takes place, let us consider four examples: Milton Keynes, Telford, Penrhys and Livingston.

Milton Keynes is different

The borough

In 1967 Milton Keynes was designated as the last of the New Towns in England. On 1 April 1997 it was vested as a new Unitary Authority. The present population of 200,000 is set to rise to 253,000 by the year 2011. The borough includes many villages and the four towns of Bletchley, Newport Pagnell, Stony Stratford and Wolverton, as well as the designated area of the New Town. Eighty per cent of the population lives in twenty per cent of the total area, the other twenty per cent being scattered in a large area of villages.

Local churches

There are a hundred churches in Milton Keynes, including about thirty independent evangelical churches, and approximately seventy others which are members of the Milton Keynes Christian Council. Some thirty churches are Grade 1 listed buildings, having been there for an average of 700 years. There are also many brand new buildings including the Church of Christ the Vine (an old pub recently converted into a church), Christ the King (a fully integrated Roman Catholic, Methodist, United Reformed, Baptist and Anglican LEP), the Church of the Servant King, which is also a community centre (as is Trinity Church in Fishermead), the Church of the Holy Cross in Two Mile Ash, Water Eaton Church Centre, Hodge Lea, Whaddon Way, the Cross and Stable in Downs Barn, the Salvation Army in Conniburrow, the Quaker Centre in Downs Barn and the Church of Christ the Cornerstone in the city centre, again shared by the five main denominations.

Of the seventy churches in the Christian Council, twenty-three are Local Ecumenical Partnerships and, with one or two exceptions, these are grouped into five ecumenical parishes.

Beginnings

This all came about through the foresight of Harry Carpenter, Anglican Bishop of Oxford, Charles Grant, Roman Catholic Bishop of Northampton, Douglas Hicks, Baptist Area Superintendent, A. Kingsley Turner, Methodist District Chairman and John White, Congregational Moderator, who formed an Inter-Church Committee in 1967. By 1969 there was a Joint Churches Working Party under the chairmanship of the Anglican Bishop of Buckingham and, by 1970, a set of ecumenical proposals had been incorporated as a substantial section in the Development

Corporation's two volume 'Master Plan'. A special Lent course on 'City and Church', to explain what was going on, attracted an attendance of over 700!

Ecumenical parishes

Many new church sites were selected, only one of which remains to be built on. The decision was taken to remove the boundaries of Anglican parishes and create extended ecumenical parishes, in which a few local churches would be grouped together as ecumenical congregations with the development of ecumenical councils and ministerial teams. There are now five ecumenical parishes, namely Woughton (five churches; three Anglican, one Methodist, one URC ministers), Walton (three churches; two Anglican, one Baptist, one Roman Catholic ministers), Watling Valley (five churches; three Anglican, one URC ministers), Stantonbury (eight churches; six Anglican, one Baptist, one Methodist ministers), City Centre Parish of the Church of Christ the Cornerstone (two Anglican, two Roman Catholic, one Methodist, one URC ministers). The Baptist, Methodist and United Reformed Church ministers are Free Church Ministers representing all three denominations.

Sector ministries

Since the beginning the work of the churches has developed not only at the local church and parish level, but in a variety of sector ministries. The Education Sector was established in 1970 and, by way of a series of reincarnations, has now been developed as the Milton Keynes Training Commission based at The Well at Willen. Apart from a wide variety of courses such as banner workshops, drama, gospel studies and exploration of spiritualities, there is an eight-module clergy induction programme, as well as the three-year Milton Keynes Christian Training Course offering training in the bible, worship, the Church, spirituality, theology, church history and much more. This course is recognized ecumenically as being suitable for the training of URC, Methodist and Baptist lay preachers and Anglican lay readers.

The Industrial Sector well illustrates the ecumenical nature of Milton Keynes. Beginning in 1971 with the appointment of Trevor Dale, a Methodist, there has been a whole series of Industrial and City Centre chaplains. Of particular note was the launching in 1983 of 'CROP' – a Community Recycling Opportunities Programme – on the Kiln Farm Industrial Estate. With a starting capital of £38 in the bank, CROP now has an annual turnover of £6 million and has been handed over to Milton Keynes Council. For several years Robert Brown, a Baptist, who was funded by the Anglican Oxford Diocesan Industrial Board, was responsible for CROP. The present City Centre Chaplain, David Moore, is financed by the Oxford Diocese and the Industrial Chaplain, Ian Parker, linked to specific industries such as Abbey National, is paid by the Methodist Connection.

The Christian Foundation is a very important part of the sector ministry. In the very early days the Anglican Planning Officer convened regular meetings of the sector ministers, including those involved in social responsibility and youth work. By 1982 an integrated team, with a unified management, was in being and it developed the concept of a Christian Foundation with an emphasis on education through experience. Using Methodist and URC buildings and with Baptist, Salvation Army, Methodist and URC personnel, the foundation was supported with Anglican money and inspired by the vision of Veronica Conner, a Roman Catholic sister from the Society of the Holy Child Jesus. The new premises of the Christian Foundation were opened by Dr Phyllis Starkey MP on 8 October, 1997. Work on a new scheme to provide sixteen bed-sits for young people aged 17–25 has just begun, linked with training to assist the residents to make the transition to independent living. The Foundation has been instrumental in the development of the Wolverton Partnership for the regeneration of Wolverton, which has received a government award of £1.3 million. Apart from the improvement of the physical environment, the money will provide a new childcare facility; create a range of training opportunities; improve town centre security; and support local businesses. Funds are being raised for a Rent Deposit Guarantee Scheme for those in need of housing and there is extended training for persistent non-attenders from local schools, to the extent of about sixty per year. A vegetarian restaurant called Eating Point is run on Stantonbury Campus.

Altogether there are some thirty people involved in sector ministry in Milton Keynes, including hospital and prison chaplains, outreach work in secondary schools, chaplaincies with police and ambulance services and much more. All this work is greatly enhanced by the fact that it is done, and seen to be done, ecumenically.

The Milton Keynes Christian Council

The Council has a history going back to July 1968, when it began life as the Ecumenical Committee. By 1971, it was known as the Christian Council. A recent suggestion to rename it Churches Together for Milton Keynes was resisted by the denominational church leaders on the grounds that it was a far more cohesive and effective body than most Churches Together groups. In 1981 Gethin Abraham-Williams, a Baptist minister, became the first Ecumenical Officer of the Council; in 1984 the leaders of the Roman Catholic, Methodist, Church of England, Baptist and United Reformed churches (now known as the Presidents) signed a public Declaration of Commitment, and in 1990 Hugh Cross, another Baptist minister, was appointed Ecumenical Moderator. In 1996 he was succeeded by Murdoch MacKenzie from the United Reformed Church.

The role of the Ecumenical Moderator is to exercise visionary and pastoral ecumenical leadership; to focus and symbolize in a personal way the unity of the Christian community in the Borough of Milton Keynes; to help the Christian community to relate to the civic community, to challenge the denominational structures to engage increasingly in joint decision-making in the pursuit of their common mission; and to share in developing an emerging ministry of oversight, not necessarily modelled upon that of any one of the participating denominations. Each of the five denominations has laid out its particular understanding of what the Ecumenical Moderator might do on its behalf, which includes a relationship of mutual confidence, a teaching ministry and, in particular, the pastoral care of clergy and religious.

The Presidents meet three times a year, as does the Ecumenical Assembly, presided over by the Lay Chair. The main work of the Council is expressed in the life of the local churches and the various sector ministries. There is also an Administrator and a series of commissions and committees which help to service the churches' work. Thus Milton Keynes is different in so far as it has one of the most closely integrated ecumenical arrangements in England.

Telford stands like a beacon

In the foreword to the Annual Report 1996–7 of the Telford Christian Council, Rt Revd David Hallatt, Anglican Bishop of Shrewsbury, writes:

> *The work of the Telford Christian Council is not only very encouraging, but stands as a beacon to the wider Church of all denominations. It is a picture to all of us of wonderful co-operation and collaboration, an effective sign of the fulfilment in our midst of our Lord's prayer . . . that they may be one, that the world may believe.*

History and development

Over many years the work of the Council was led and inspired by Colin Hill and the effectiveness and range of this work is indicated by the fact that the annual financial turnover for 1996 was over £600,000. As early as 1963, the New Town of Dawley was designated and the then church leaders met as the Area Interdenominational Committee. In 1968 the area was re-designated as Telford New Town and the Development Corporation looked for working alliances with the churches, if they would co-operate ecumenically. In 1972 the local churches formed the Telford Christian Council and in the mid 1980s the Area Interdenominational Committee and the Telford Christian Council merged. At present David Lavender is the Development Officer for Mission and Ministry and heads the team of seven ecumenical officers, which includes a Director of Community Projects, a Bookshop Manager, a Youth Chaplain, a Town Centre Chaplain and a Churches Industrial Officer. Roman Catholics, Anglicans, Methodists, United Reformed, Quakers, Baptists and the Salvation Army work together in a whole range of community projects, as well as through over eighty local churches.

In 1996 Telford Christian Council adopted the following Mission Statement:

> *The Telford Christian Council is a coming together of Christian Churches in and around Telford. We seek to discover God at work in the world and to share in his work. We aim to listen to our changing society and engage with it, so as to:*
> - *encourage and work for reconciliation and wholeness, the relief of deprivation and responsible participation in family life, the local community, economic and political life.*
> - *challenge and enable member churches to be an effective sign of unity to the wider church and community.*
> - *assist churches to celebrate and proclaim the good news of God as revealed in Jesus Christ.*

The Council's work falls under three headings:

1. Encouraging local Associations of Churches in their work.
2. Working in partnership with them and other agencies to provide a number of projects of supported accommodation for homeless young people, and other community projects.
3. Providing a number of townwide ministries through the Ecumenical Officers.

Encouraging local Associations of Churches

The churches of the Telford area are grouped into seven Associations (Councils of Churches), with a great variety of work:

Oakengates and Donnington Association of Churches

On Advent Sunday our churches closed their evening services to meet at St George's Parish Church for an Advent Carol Service. The theme was 'The light of the world'. Despite this being a new event, over 250 people attended! The Holiday Club held in Wombridge Park each August started some years ago as an event organized by a single church trying to reach out to its local community. A number of churches now work together to run this evangelistic event for local children and their families.

Central Telford Ecumenical Partnership

1996 was a milestone year in the development of the Partnership. In July we celebrated the first ten years of Anglicans and Methodists working together in the Partnership. We held a united service for all ten partnership churches at St Leonard's, Malinslee, and letters of commendation were read out from other church leaders, including our Telford Christian Council President. This was also a public forum to reaffirm our commitment by issuing each church with a framed copy of our Vision Statement for our future work.

Newport Christian Council

1996 has proved to be a busy year. The seven Lent groups organized by the Newport Christian Council were well attended with over sixty participants. There are also ongoing activities in the area which Newport Christian Council seeks to support. These include: the Youth Café, where financial as well as volunteer help is offered; Mike Taylor's 'Shropshire Cares' charity, which we helped found; the 'Newport for One World' group, of which we are a part; and close links with the local Christian Aid Group. The Iona Group is also an active participant in our Council.

Churches Together in Shifnal

Churches Together in Shifnal was formally founded on St Andrew's Day 1994 with a service of Commitment at St Andrew's Church. The churches had been working together before this date, but this service marked a significant move towards a greater working and sharing together. Since then the work that had already begun has taken on a great sense of direction and focus. Churches Together in Shifnal includes the Church of England, Methodist and Catholic churches in the town, plus the six country parishes under the leadership of Revd David Chantrey. All play their part in this work of co-operation and sharing. It is encouraging to see how our work has developed, with shared events such as united Lent Group meetings and Lent Lunches, which began last year and proved very successful. It is good that our Christmas witness has been strengthened with the united Christmas card sent from the churches throughout the town. There is also greater participation at the Open Air Community Carol Service on Christmas Eve. With the help of all the clergy and the Salvation Army band, this proved to be a major community event.

Wellington and District Association of Churches

The undoubted highlight of 1996 was the celebration of our 25th anniversary. The Association was inaugurated as long ago as 1971. The celebration, in the form of an Ecumenical Service of confession, thanksgiving and commitment, took place on Sunday, 29 September in New Street Methodist Church. It was very well supported by members of all churches. All the Churches in the Association also signed a Declaration of Intent to govern their future working together.

South Telford Association of Churches

Throughout the past year a great deal of prayer and planning has gone into the development of the worshipping community in Woodside, an area of social deprivation. The congregation that

meets in the Community Centre there each week is growing and,
with the arrival of Revd Jonathan Fox as team vicar, it is hoped to
develop a practical ecumenical partnership to provide ministry
and mission. A highlight of 1996 was the Association's annual
meeting. Such was the success of the evening that the various
young people's groups decided to meet together again in October to celebrate All Saints Eve with a Light Fantastic Party,
which provided a fine Christian alternative to Hallowe'en.

Community and homeless projects

The STAY Project continues its crucial role in responding to
those who are homeless in an emergency, with nearly 1,200 refer-
rals made during 1996. The pressure has been on the Accommodation Bureau to identify numerous ranges of accommodation. A
particular difficulty is the placing of 16 to 17-year-olds. The con-
tingency fund set up by the Telford Religious Society of Friends
continues to be greatly used, with various groups contributing to
it.

New developments include the recent purchase of the former
TSB Bank in Oakengates. This will provide additional accom-
modation for those moving out of STAY's emergency provision.
It will consist of four flats, an office and a retail unit.

At Blews Hill Court, we are glad to see two volunteers, one an
ex-tenant, joining the salaried staff. It is a real inspiration being
involved in the Watling Community Centre, a joint project between Wellington Association of Churches and Wrekin Council.
The centre is well used and is a credit to those involved.

Newstart

Over the last four years Telford Christian Council has been
working with the Stonham Housing Association towards becoming an 'arm's length' managing agent for Stonham's provision for homeless people within the District. This happened on 1
April 1996 and, with the aid of an injection of money from both
Wrekin Council and Telford Christian Council, we have been

able to change shared space into self-contained rooms. This has transformed the living conditions for residents in our Malinslee accommodation and makes it possible to accommodate males and females. With Stonham's help, we hope in the near future to be able to transform conditions at the Madeley house too.

Manor Heights Community Project

1996 was a year of considerable change in the Manor Heights Community Project. New staff were employed and new duties taken on. During 1997, work was done on the Community flat to enlarge and improve facilities.

Chairs and Spares

Chairs and Spares continues to operate in conjunction with Manor Heights Community Project. In July 1996 the Chairs and Spares store moved into new premises near Manor Heights and we now encourage anyone in the Wrekin area who is in receipt of benefit to call at the store any Saturday morning, bringing with them proof of benefit and some identification. They can purchase items of furniture at minimal prices, which are then delivered to them.

Telford Christian Council's ministries

One for the Kingdom

This is a new initiative which aims to help Christians in Telford to learn from each other's traditions of worship and experience of being Christian communities. The idea is quite simple: different congregations from different Christian traditions and areas of Telford are invited to lead worship in the ecumenical chapel of Christ the King. Each monthly service has attracted forty to fifty people, with a very useful time for questions and discussion afterwards.

For God's Sake . . . Unity

Town Centre Ministry

Peter Cope continues to visit the staff at Asda, Boots and C&A every four weeks or so, and endeavours to foster a sense of community amongst the store managers through the Traders Association. Regular visiting of police headquarters at Malinsgate gives rise to some important conversations. Six Faith and Work sessions have been organized for a group of town centre employees and lively Christian worship has been brought to the shopping malls in the first series of Shoppers Services to be held in Telford Town Centre on some Sundays before Christmas.

Officer for Industry and Commerce

A grant has been given by Industry 96 to make a video-based course for church home groups. The course has five sessions and looks at both the good and bad effects of industry in the light of Christian faith. Attention will be given to women at work. Telford, like Shropshire as a whole, is a low pay area for both men and women.

Youth chaplaincy

The past year has seen some groups building on past successes, others experiencing painful rebirth after older members, and sometimes leaders, move on. Telford currently has between twelve and fifteen local church youth groups. We are planning a churches' youth tent at Telford's annual Kids International Festival. Called KIPPERS, it will host a rolling programme over the two-day event, with live music and drama and some Christian youth work around the festival site. (It was a great success in 1997!).

Revelations bookshop

For Telford Christian Council's Christian bookshop, 1996 was a very hard year as far as business was concerned. We really do need support from the local churches to enable us to give the best possible service.

Volunteers, administration and personnel

Volunteers play a very important part in all areas of Telford Christian Council's work. In particular, we rely on volunteers to staff our two Wear Next community shops and Revelations bookshop. Since we set up a database of our volunteers and included our various management committees, the numbers have increased to 151! There are now fifty-five staff employed at the Christian Council's various sites throughout the town. Many of these are part-time and some are seconded from denominations to work with us.

Supporting committee structure

Working with seven major national denominations is bound to be complex, as is working with the number and variety of the projects described above. Among the many different management and advisory committees involved, the Telford Christian Council Advisory Committee should be mentioned as the meeting of regional church leaders to provide guidance and support for the whole of the Council's work. The Executive Committee meets monthly; it consists of representatives of denominations and Associations of Churches, and supervises much of the Council's continuing work. The Sponsoring Committee monitors and supports the nine Local Ecumenical Partnerships in Telford

Penrhys: the story of Llanfair in Wales

The Council of Churches for Wales was established in 1956. A national faith and order conference was held in 1963 on the theme 'The unity we seek'. Together with Nottingham 1964, this led ultimately in 1974 to five of the member churches of the Council covenanting towards visible union. The churches involved were the Church in Wales, the Methodist Church, the Presbyterian Church of Wales, the United Reformed Church and twelve congregations of the Baptist Union of Great Britain in South Wales. In 1976 ENFYS, the Commission of the

Covenanted Churches, was set up to foster the covenant locally and nationally.

In 1990 CYTUN, Churches Together in Wales, was established as a successor to the Council of Churches for Wales. It works in collaboration with ENFYS and with the Free Church Council of Wales, and has an Assembly, Y Gymanfa, which meets once every two years. This collaboration supports about 130 local CYTUN/Churches Together groups and something approaching a hundred Local Ecumenical Partnerships.[8]

Llanfair, Penrhys, Rhondda

Penrhys is an ancient site, standing where the roads of prehistoric people met. The great ridge roads were joined by a track on the saddle across Penrhys, which served to connect these roads and the river fords across the two Rhondda rivers. Just below the Penrhys ridge is a well which dates from pre-history and was 'Christianized' by Celtic monks. This area of North Glamorgan is associated with three Celtic saints: Illtud, Gwynno and Tyfodwg. Their settlements were known as a 'llan', which referred both to a building and a community. For over 300 years in the Middle Ages, Penrhys was served by Cistercian monks who tended the Shrine of Our Lady of Penrhys. Thousands of pilgrims came to receive water from the ancient well and to pray at the statue on the brow of the hill. In 1538 the Reformers removed the statue and burned it. In 1953 a new statue was erected and blessed. The new chapel at Penrhys is called Llanfair: Mary's Community, Mary's settlement, Mary's people.

In 1851 less than a thousand people lived in Rhondda. Within sixty years, 170,000 arrived. By 1984 it was down to 80,000. In 1914 there were 151 nonconformist chapels; today there are less than half that number. In Tylorstown (the nearest village to Penrhys), there were eight chapels with two thousand members. Today there is one chapel with less than a dozen worshippers.

Till the 1960s, Penrhys was the home of a farm, sheep, skylarks and courting couples – a place of peace. Due to the excesses of 1960s' planners, Penrhys today, perched on a mountain ridge, has

333333333

a thousand dwellings on sites rising from 1,000 to 1,350 feet. Of its population of three thousand, 93 per cent are unemployed, 90 per cent are on housing benefits, 37 per cent are under the age of fourteen and there are large numbers of single parents. Its population now, in 1998, has declined to about 1,200; and nearly four hundred properties have been demolished.

A table that is round

In 1971 the chapel in Penrhys was founded as an Interdenominational Fellowship in which all the eight churches of the Council of Churches for Wales participated. In September 1989 there were ten adults and twenty children in the congregation. In that year a new ecumenical experiment was launched with a new pattern of life. In 1992 a derelict block of flats was converted into Llanfair, Mary's community, the House of Magnificat. Now more than fifty adults and the same number of children worship or are in Sunday School each week. A bi-monthly Church and Project Meeting decides on issues relating to the local church and to projects. A sponsoring body, made up of representatives from the eight denominations (appointed by the national church bodies) and the local church, meets three times a year.

Every child in the Penrhys schools worships regularly in what is seen as their community church. Llanfair includes a music room, a nearly new clothes boutique, a launderette, a homework centre, a cafe, a crèche and a chapel. In the centre is a round communion table and the spirit of Llanfair is illustrated by the words of Fred Kaan's hymn:

> *The church is like a table*
> *set in an open house;*
> *no protocol for seating,*
> *a symbol of inviting,*
> *of sharing, drinking, eating;*
> *an end to 'them' and 'us'.*

A second stage of the work has developed within the Penrhys Partnership, with the carving of an amphitheatre out of the hillside and the development of a village centre with a new health centre, food co-operative and credit union This was followed by the opening of a block of flats for the more vulnerable (Centre F, 1995) and an arts centre (Canolfan Rhys, 1997).

At the heart of all this is a small international community led by John and Norah Morgans. Approximately seven in number, they live together 'above the shop' and have both a deep involvement in the local community and a world-wide network of ecumenical friends. A fascinating account of the Penrhys Llanfair story is found in *Penrhys: The Story of Llanfair* by John I. Morgans.[10] It is a story of which George MacLeod would have approved, in which the household of the world finds its touchstone in the *nearest church.*

Livingston Ecumenical Parish in Scotland

LEPs are much fewer in Scotland. This reflects the greater numerical strength of congregations of the Church of Scotland and the uneven spread of the smaller denominations.

However, there are, apart from Livingston, a number of LEPs whose influence, given Scotland's smaller population, has proved and is continuing to prove significant. Grahamston United Church in Falkirk with two Church of Scotland, one Congregational and one Methodist congregations was established in 1972. A fully integrated congregation, with one set of buildings since 1984, it has a united membership of 750. It is governed by a basis of association because lawyers believe that to become a united church could be tantamount to forming a new denomination. Lay leadership and pastoral care are integrated. There are part-time Methodist and Congregational ministers and a full-time Church of Scotland minister.

Morningside United in Edinburgh, with 350 members, brought together one Church of Scotland and one Congregational church in the early 1970s. There the legal problem has been overcome by their being treated as congregations of the Church of Scotland and the Congregational Church simultaneously. The more recent Augustine United Church in Edinburgh is a union of congregations of the United Reformed Church and the Scottish Congregational Church. There has been informal sharing between St Cuthbert's and St. John's in Edinburgh's West End, the Murrayfield churches, also in Edinburgh, and Church of Scotland and Episcopalians in Kinloch Rannoch and in Mid Craigie in Dundee. Congregationalists and Methodists have formed a uniting church in Mosspark in Glasgow, while Thornhill in Dumfriesshire has had Congregational and Church of Scotland sharing for twenty years or more.

Oakshaw Trinity Paisley is an integrated congregation of three Church of Scotland churches and one Congregational. It began with a shared community café and social welfare project and now has a team of three ministers who share pastoral responsibility, but constitutionally and legally belong to both denominations simultaneously. It was their petition to the Church of Scotland General Assembly which led to the Act allowing ministers of other denominations legally to moderate at Kirk Session meetings in an ecumenical project. There are also a number of other places in which some sharing of church buildings takes place.

Livingston Ecumenical Parish

The main area of ecumenical sharing in Scotland has been in Livingston New Town, which now has a population of fifty thousand. Of the eight denominations participating in the Scottish Faith and Order Conference in 1963, three of them, the Church of Scotland, the Scottish Episcopal Church and the Congregational Union of Scotland, agreed to designate the New Town of Livingston as 'an area of ecumenical experiment'. They were joined by the Methodists in 1968. St Columba's was built by the Church of Scotland, St Paul's by the Scottish Episcopal Church and the Congregational Union built the church and community complex known as the Lanthorn. Much later, in 1989, the Methodists signed the lease on the Mosswood Community Centre. By 1984 all the properties of the Ecumenical Experiment were seen as shared responsibility. Lastly, in 1994, a new building was opened at Nether Dechmont, known as the Carmondean Church.

By 1975 a team of six ministers worked together – two Church of Scotland, two Episcopal, one Congregational and a Methodist Deaconess. By 1978 the Church of Scotland had appointed a Community Minister and the General Assembly agreed to allow Church of Scotland ministers to exercise their ministerial functions throughout the whole area of the Ecumenical Experiment.

The Livingston Ecumenical Council met for the first time in October 1970 and in 1984 became the Ecumenical Parish Council. A new Basis and Plan of Union takes effect from 1 January, 1998, which will, in effect, give the ecumenical parish its first proper constitution. By 1996 the number of ministers had been reduced to three, working throughout the area. In the midst of all this, over the past thirty years, the work of the churches has been of great significance, especially in the areas of youth work, community development and social caring, much of which has been pioneered by the Livingston Ecumenical Parish. During 1997 an in-depth evaluation of youth work raised the possibility of employing a town-wide, ecumenical youth worker in collaboration with the other denominations which exist in Livingston.

The tip of the iceberg

The four examples given above are simply the tip of an iceberg. This is particularly true in England, where each of the 800 Local Ecumenical Partnerships is unique. They range from the elaborate examples of Milton Keynes and Telford to the situation in the three parishes of Helsington, Levens and Underbarrow in Cumbria, where a lay preacher of the United Reformed Church, at the request of the people of the parishes, is licensed to preach by the Anglican bishop. More recently, a possible 'Declaration of Ecumenical Welcome and Commitment by a Church of England Parish' has been issued. It is intended for use in communities where the sole church building and worshipping community is the parish church, which also provides a home for Christians of many different traditions. Another example is the small rural village of West Bretton in the Wakefield Diocese, where Anglicans and Methodists have come together in a Methodist building.[11] Variations on these themes are endless, but each of them enables local Christians to worship in their nearest church, regardless of its denomination!

And finally . . .

If the *nearest local church* working ecumenically for everyone is to be the touchstone of the Good News, what do local people feel about such ecumenical partnerships? What is best about them? What are the greatest difficulties? What are their hopes for the future? The following are some results of a recent sample.

Best things

'Sharing of worship, resources, finance and clergy.' 'The town sees we are together.' 'Being pioneers after centuries of division.' 'Openness/flexible/more informal/friendly/less institutional.' 'Celebrating our Covenant each year, using the Methodist Covenant Service.' 'Greater lay participation.' 'Learning new ways of worship and pastoral care.'

Difficulties

'Keeping four denominations happy with forms, administration, etc.' 'The thought of going back to one denomination after leaving the LEP.' 'Time taken for decisions.' 'Lack of commitment to the vision by some clergy.' 'Parochialism and the tendency towards an inward-looking mentality.' 'Helping members of individual Christian congregations to look beyond their own membership, concerns and culture to the needs of the whole community of Christians – what each can give, and what each can receive.' 'Battling against the institutional thinking and inertia of all Christian denominations. Changing this is truly a work of the Spirit!' 'Arranging a joint confirmation service was difficult in the early days, but in recent times this problem has been overcome.' 'For a small village ecumenical congregation, representation at denominational meetings, Circuit/Deanery, can prove difficult sometimes.'

Hopes for the future

'That new people moving into the parish may feel there is a place for them in their local church, rather than going into the town.' 'That increasing numbers of Christians will see that their discipleship and spiritual lives are incomplete, unless they are in relationship with, and learning from, the whole range of Christian traditions which surround them.' 'That the British churches will set definite targets on the road to visible unity.' 'Full sharing of the Eucharist.' 'Increasing number of ecumenical parishes, so others can enjoy the benefits.' 'Greater Roman Catholic involvement.'

All of this is a response by people who seek to love God on the one hand and their neighbour on the other. Their global ecumenical vision is translated into down-to-earth practical action, as they seek that unity for which Christ prayed in obedience to the will of the living God.

NOTES

1. Prepared by a group from Churches Together in England, *Called to be One* (CTE Publications, 1996) pp. 13–29.
2. Lesslie Newbigin, *The Gospel in a Pluralist Society* (SPCK, London, 1989) p.222ff.
3. Jill Evans, *The Ecumenical Scene* (Hereford Diocesan Ecumenical Committee; £1.25 including postage).
4. David Butler, *Dying to be One* (SCM Press, London, 1996) p.145.
5. Ibid., p.148.
6. Elizabeth Welch and Flora Winfield, *Travelling Together* (CTE Publications, London, 1995) p.vii.
7. Roger Nunn, *This Growing Unity* (CTE Publications, London, 1995).
8. Elizabeth Welch and Flora Winfield, op. cit., p.8ff.
9. Fred Kaan, *Rejoice and Sing* (Oxford University Press for the URC, Oxford, 1991), hymn 480.
10. John I. Morgans, *Penrhys: The Story of Llanfair* (June, 1994)
11. Leonard Bartle, *The Church in West Bretton* (April, 1997)

Seven

FOR THE WORLD'S SAKE ... UNITY
Maxwell Craig

> *God was in Christ, reconciling the world to himself.*
> *(2 Corinthians 5.19)*

Reconciliation is a formidable task. Whether it is nations or neighbours, employers or employees, chairpersons or churches, we are all tempted to put reconciliation in the 'too difficult' tray on our desk or workbench. It means taking the risk of humiliation if that crucial first step is spurned. Public relations consultants do not like the word. A fourteen-letter word, they say, cannot serve as an effective slogan. Yet reconciliation is at the heart of the Christian gospel. It is in joint harness with forgiveness, is indeed the necessary preliminary to, and outworking of, forgiveness. If we are wary of a fourteen-letter word, we can prefer its paraphrase – 'making friends out of enemies', 'turning enemies into friends'. I shall argue in this chapter that the unity the Christian Church is called to promote within its own life is not for its own sake, but for the world's sake. Jesus prayed ' . . . that they may all be one. Father, may they be in us, just as you are in me and I in you. May they be one, so that the world will believe that you sent me.' (John 17.21, *Good News Bible*).

South Africa and apartheid

27 April, 1994, was, for me, the day of the century. That long-awaited election day marked the birth of democracy in South Africa. On that day apartheid died and a new world was born. No real birth is easy. President Nelson Mandela, perhaps the world's number one hero, has a minefield of long-delayed hopes across which to lead his people. Water and electric power are

being made available to the people of the townships, but expectations far outstrip their provision. Pretoria's Truth and Reconciliation Commission has no doubt made mistakes; but it remains one of the world's most remarkable attempts to replace hatred with forgiveness and look to a genuinely harmonious future. Hope still stirs strong in South Africa and the churches have made, and continue to make, a notable contribution.

The contribution of the churches during the pre-election period repays the telling. In 1992 the South African Council of Churches approached the World Council of Churches. In their approach they said:

> *Ours is a violent country. Between now and the election day we will have outbreaks of violence. Can the world's churches send teams of men and women to live beside us and visit our townships and stand alongside us during these dangerous days? If they come, they will demonstrate that the enterprise in which we are engaged is one which is close to the heart of God and is being anxiously watched by his Church throughout the world.*

Over the next two years groups of men and women came and saw and shared the joy that concluded the 'long walk to freedom' that conquered apartheid.

I had the privilege of spending the five weeks leading up to the election acting as a 'peace monitor' on behalf of the World Council of Churches. Our mission was set out to the whole group who assembled in Johannesburg at the end of March 1994. That mission was to divide ourselves into teams of four and live in the community to which each team was assigned; to make contact with the whole range of people from local government officers, police and trade union officials, through local Afrikaner landowners, to clergy and community representatives in the townships; to worship in black and white churches; to attend political rallies and voter education events; and, during the election itself, to be present at as many as possible of the large number of voting stations in our area. The four of us, from

Kenya, Norway, Eire and Scotland, were posted to the gold-mining and agricultural part of the Western Transvaal. We monitored thirty-two voting stations on those three tumultuous days. They were called voting stations because the term 'polling stations' sounded too much like 'police stations' at a time when the police were often thought to be electorally suspect.

Four years on, I can still see the resolute determination of people of all ages to cast their vote for the first time in their lives. The young wheelchair-bound woman who had to be lifted over a turnstile, wheelchair and all, to gain entry into the voting station – and laughed throughout the cumbersome procedure. The wrinkled wee woman who scorned to vote on the special day set aside for the elderly and infirm, because she wanted to queue with everyone else – she was 97! The burly Afrikaner, a local farmer, who drove his truck to the voting station ferrying fifty-three people to the polls, knowing very well that they would all be likely to vote for the African National Congress. He did it with a smiling grace. The song throughout the townships was 'Nkosi Sikelel' iAfrika – God Bless Africa'. God did indeed bless Africa during those miraculous days.

To those of us who saw him during that whole period, as to millions throughout the world, Nelson Mandela was a symbol of reconciling grace. He is also an astute politician. I remember a 45,000-strong rally at the Orlando Stadium in Soweto which he attended. The programme of music and singing and speeches which had gone on all day was raucously interrupted by shouts of acclamation – Mandela had arrived! His car drove slowly round the circuit of the stadium, allowing him to greet each section of the crowd. The response was electric. But the natural politician in him knew that was not enough. He then got out of the car and walked slowly and deliberately round the perimeter of the race-track, as close to the crowd as he could get, smiling and greeting and raising his arm in the ANC salute. This was an astonishing risk. There were hundreds of weapons in the stadium that day, some in the hands of 12 and 13-year-olds, most barely hidden.

From the security of our churches, it is easy to talk the language of reconciliation. Of course the churches must speak that language, in season and out of season. It is their sacred commission. But it is expected; it is predictable; it surprises no one. When a man has spent twenty-seven years of his life in prison on an unjust charge, in the harsh conditions of Robben Island, and when that same man can extend the hand of friendship to the leader of the government which kept him in prison, there grow the seeds of something new and full of hope. When that man speaks of reconciliation, the world listens. But even this very genuine listening does not seem able to effect at international level the transformation which, painfully and with many a setback to come, South Africa is achieving.

The curse of Babel

Why is international harmony so elusive? The Babel episode (Genesis 11.1–9) tells the story. Armed with a single language and the means for their purpose, the people of the earth resolve 'to make a name for themselves'. Their purpose was their own gratification, giving no place to God. The power and the glory were to be theirs, with no thought given to the purpose of creation or the honouring of the creator. We see Babel rehearsed in every generation. A man walking on the moon? Yes – to demonstrate American power; to punish the Soviet Union's temerity in being the first into space with their sputnik; to provide a twentieth-century circus to court popular approval in true Roman Emperor style.

In the film *Field of Dreams*, Kevin Costner plays an obsessive baseball fan. To bolster his obsession he has money, lots of it. So he builds a huge baseball stadium out in the desert region of Arizona. There are no crowds to watch the game or fill the stadium; nor any teams to play the game. It is a monument to an obsession. Some of the millennial ideas currently being considered are the same. The Greenwich Dome, with a very limited future and continuing uncertainty about its content, at a cost of £750 million. The biggest Ferris wheel you have ever seen, twice the size of Big Ben, is planned for the Thames – and it does not even tell the time. A tower is planned for London, the biggest in the world it was to be; now Paris has trumped it with a bigger one. All these notions have to carry superlatives – the broadest, the most lavish, the biggest, the highest. They express the muscle of money; they are part of the economic strait-jacket into which market forces have compressed us.

What follows from an idolatry like this? It is not too difficult to find the words. We should call it Babel and read the eleventh chapter of Genesis again. This would help us to see that what the market does is to dethrone the living God and put a god of gold and silver in his place. The Babel we have built has bricks of dollars, yen, marks and pounds sterling. We worship that Babel each morning as we hear reports of the money markets, how the yen is moving against the dollar and what the mark has done to sterling.

If this idolatrous catalogue started and ended with money, it would be bad enough. But the result is much more dangerous. Build a Babel of gold or dollars and you need an army to protect it; build a palace at Kinshasa, when the bulk of your people live in corrugated iron or hard-board shacks, and you need an army to protect it; build a society which measures its success by its gross domestic product and the interest rate and condemns 15 per cent of its people to a life that is not a true part of the life of the community, and you need a Jubilee to solve it. Because the Old Testament valued people made in the image of God, they had to do something very positive to break the chains of slavery. That was the impetus behind the Jubilee proposal in the Old Testament book of Leviticus. Today's slavery is unemployment. That is why the argument about European Monetary Union should arrest our attention. Is the creation of jobs more important than launching EMU in 1999 or not? That is an issue more appropriate for economists and more precisely about timing, because we shall have monetary union in Europe in due course. Slavery, whether physical or economic, is a far deeper problem.

The real answer to slavery is Jubilee – to cancel debt, promote 'good work' and restore property to those who, through folly, laziness or sheer bad luck, have lost it. Jubilee 2000 is the right goal for the Church because it has no time for the Ferris wheel or the Greenwich Dome or the Babel of the Millennium, but goes to the heart of the matter. A just society, which abhors slavery, needs no armies. That is the vital importance of Jubilee 2000 and the cancellation of international debt.

International debt

When I was a boy and my father needed a loan from the bank, he put on his best suit, stuffed his briefcase with character references and walked with respectful step to his appointment with the manager. The somewhat grudging interview which followed was one of a suppliant asking a favour of a hard-nosed defender of banking rectitude. A set of similar scenes would have graced most banks until the late 1960s. Since then, the transformation has been total. Banks are keen to scatter barely guaranteed loans as widely as they can; bank managers now plead with customers to take on bigger and bigger loans. In a word, debt has become respectable – provided you are in work, look healthy and came to the bank in your car.

What made the change? Perhaps an important factor was the relaxation of banking limits. At one time, a bank would have, say, assets in its vaults of £1 million. It could therefore lend happily up to that limit. Over the years, the need for restraint was judged to be less pressing. It is now widely accepted that if a bank has assets of £1 million, it can lend up to £8 million. It only requires hard assets of 12½ per cent of the total sum it intends to lend. Where does this extra £7 million come from? Is it real money? There is a great deal of 'unreal money' awash within our economic structures. Extrapolate this situation on to the international stage and you have the makings of disaster.

One important difference between my personal borrowing and the debt of a country is that I can go bankrupt, but a country cannot. Because a lender, whether bank or other business, knows that I can go bankrupt, he takes a measure of responsibility and indeed a degree of risk in his decision to offer a loan. There is a conscious sharing, both of the responsibility and of the risk.
152

When the prospective debtor is a country, there is no risk and little sense of responsibility on the part of the lender. Add to this dangerous situation the events of the early 1970s, when the government of the USA flooded the world's economies with petrodollars, together with the increase in the price of oil, and you have banks even more keen to offer loans. They found themselves the recipients of vast amounts of dollars hungry for use, at a time when the developing countries were easy targets for loans. The banks made these offers with little expectation of early repayment. This, in a nutshell, described the potential for the enormity of international debt as it threatened the world's poorest countries twenty years ago. Recent years have demonstrated the devastating extent to which those least able to protect themselves have been targeted. Having accepted loans from the World Bank, the debtors are naturally required either to repay the loans or to pay the interest in order to service the loans. As the officers of the World Bank and the International Monetary Fund know very well, for the poorest countries repayment is impossible and servicing the loans virtually impossible. Mozambique, for example, has a projected budget of which 33 per cent is committed to servicing its international debt, leaving a meagre 8 per cent for education and 3 per cent for health care. Similar examples can be quoted throughout the countries of sub-Saharan Africa. When a country is required to earmark for servicing debt ten times what it plans to spend on health care, it is not surprising that the figure for infant mortality in that country is desperately high. International debt is killing children.

The issue of international debt has evoked a united response from the churches. They have embraced the Jubilee 2000 campaign with enthusiasm. This campaign provides a good example of the contribution churches can make for the world's sake, to bring new hope for millions. It can be the churches acting in unity, for the world's sake

Hope for the hopeless

The Indonesian word for hope suggests that hope is something that breaks through our horizons. The churches have designated a sequence of special emphases in the years leading up to the Millennium: 1997 is the Year of Faith, 1998 is the Year of Hope, 1999 is the Year of Love, ending with 2000 as the Year of Jubilee. This in itself is remarkable – that the churches should plan sufficiently far ahead and do that planning together so that a concerted strategy has been worked out. Our denominational horizons have been lifted. Indeed, Jubilee is the right note with which to sing a 2000th birthday song. But birthdays are usually followed by unbirthdays. For the Jubilee to sound a convincing note in our celebration of Christ, there should be a Christ-like act to be undertaken. The cancellation of unpayable debt that Jubilee 2000 promises is precisely such a Christ-like aim. It looks to wipe the slate clean for the poorest; it offers hope to millions who have been starved of hope; it promises education, health and effective work for those who have been deprived of all three; it aims to turn what is just one world into one just world.

Centuries of Christian teaching have proved unable to stem each nation's self-promotion and to impart a sense of humility to human striving. The exploration of space will continue, because 'space is there', even though a fraction of the wealth devoted to that cause could alleviate the suffering of millions. The churches have maintained a reprehensible silence in the face of this wholesale misapplication of the world's wealth. Are the stuttering steps photographed from Mars or Saturn worth a single child dying of preventable disease? When will the curse of Babel be lifted? Is hope for those who have long been starved of it nothing more than foolish optimism?

'Folk will come from East and West and from North and South and sit at table in the Kingdom of God' (Luke 13.29). The Church rejoices in the promise of this prophecy. It sounds so clear in prospect; indeed, it is clear. We are tempted, the people of the churches, to adopt this promise as our own and believe that its embrace is peculiarly about us and people like us. Yes, there will be a table in the kingdom of heaven; and our places, praise be, are incontestably reserved for us. Why are we so confident? Because our names are in the Lamb's book of life. If that is our understanding of this passage, we may need to think again. The words are ambiguous. They do not designate church people, simply people. In other words, the table is there waiting for guests who are still to be identified. One of the recurring features of all four gospels is the tough time waiting for those who feel that the top places are reserved for them – often on the shaky ground that they have grown accustomed to being treated as top-place people, whether in the Church or in the State. If the kingdom of God is 'an upside down kingdom', then those who feel superior had better make for the end of the queue and not its head. 'Friend, come up higher' is a gospel accolade. It will not work for you, if you think you have already made it. 'Blessed are the meek . . . the poor in spirit, the oppressed.'

Perhaps the most telling gospel story, relevant to those who aspire to places at the kingdom's table, is Matthew 26 – Jesus' dramatic picture of the sheep and the goats. For me, the note that emerges most strongly from this story is the note of surprise. It is a surprise experienced by those who finish on both sides of the divide. 'Lord, when did we make such a mess of things as far as you were concerned?' We may not have been above reproach, but we were always in our pew (or in our pulpit), our offering was always up to date and our private praying has been pretty pious. The King says to them: 'Because you failed to respond to the needs you certainly saw of these brothers and sisters of mine, you failed to respond to me.' To their surprise, the kingdom's door is shut in their faces.

The surprise of the others is equal and opposite. 'Yes, we may have tried to do our bit when someone else was down, but we never dreamt that you knew anything about it. That never entered our heads.' The King will say: 'Whenever you did something for one of the least of my sisters and brothers, you did it for me . . .'

The century now ending has seen brutality and heroism in their most diverse forms. The Warsaw ghetto saw both – as did the gas chambers of Auschwitz, Belsen and the rest. From the atrocities of apartheid and Bosnia's ethnic cleansing to the hounding of refugees in Zaire, the twentieth century's record of unrestrained barbarism will test the historian's alphabet. Yet all these horrors were accompanied by uncounted acts of individual heroism. The heroism can never justify the atrocity. Both point to the world's need for reconciliation rather than revenge.

Revenge and retribution dictated much of the Versailles Treaty following World War I. The result of that vengeful settlement was social and economic chaos in much of Central Europe, sowing the seeds of the Second World War. Certainly the attempt, through the League of Nations, to build a just and fair social order was doomed. Has the United Nations been built on more lasting foundations? It is probably too early to judge.

The United Nations is an expression of the international community's desire to work together for the good of the world's people. It also affords a platform for member nations to express their unregenerate nationalism. In spite of the histrionics which can absorb so much time and energy in the UN Assembly, its many agencies, UNESCO, UNHCR, UNICEF, FAO and WHO, have achieved a great deal. They are some of the instruments through which the founding ideals of the UN were turned into action in the immediate post-1945 period. The UN peacekeeping forces, in their many places of responsibility throughout the world, combine in that vital task. The UN starts from the assumption that nations have a responsibility to look beyond their own borders. The fact that the UN is an international body implies that the various nations, all of them, form its base. It stems from a widely scattered confusion of national roots.

The world Church has a different starting point. It starts from the assumption that the Church is one. This essential unity has been disrupted over the centuries through schism on theological grounds, separation on political grounds, and parting on organizational grounds. In spite of these tragic divisions, the spiritual oneness of the whole Church is accepted by all Christians. We are one in Christ, but in the Church we are divided. The scandal of disunity is something of which most Christians are profoundly ashamed. But that sense of shame seems unable to tear down the barriers which divide us. And the doubly shameful fact is that Europe's Christians have exported their divisions to those parts of the world where European missions have been active, so that African Presbyterians sing to a different tune from that of Africa's Roman Catholics and Anglicans.

Bosnia and Northern Ireland

Europe is a continent of contrasts, from the temperate coasts of Ireland and Scotland kissed by the Gulf Stream to the continental severities, winter and summer, of central and eastern Europe. Its array of languages is bewildering; the variety in the physical appearance of European peoples suggests that, far from being a homogeneous part of the world, Europe is the product of widely different genetic forces. The geography of the continent reflects this variety from sub-arctic regions in the North to the near-tropical climates of the Costa del Sol and the southern coast of Crete. Of all the world's continents, Europe may not even be a true continent as strictly defined. It is the western appendix of Asia, with no easily defined border. A continent, according to the *Oxford English Dictionary*, is 'one of the main continuous bodies of land on the earth's surface'. Europe has still to learn its role as one of the world's melting-pots in the way that America has been for so long. Europe's tribal rivalries, which threw the nations into two world wars in this century, have not yet been exorcized. And yet Europe has been the cradle of the Christian faith.

Two of the loveliest parts of Europe are Northern Ireland and Bosnia. To travel the Antrim coast from Carrickfergus to the Giant's Causeway is a delight; to explore the spectacular valleys north east from Mostar and Sarajevo in Bosnia is a contrasting and complementary delight. But the barbarism and intractability of the tribal conflicts both in Bosnia and in Northern Ireland continue to mar the beauty of their setting.

Not all of Bosnia is mountainous or agricultural. The city of Tuzla, in Northern Bosnia, has a highly industrialized economy and a predominantly Muslim community. Partly as a result of this economic difference from other parts of Bosnia, Tuzla has managed to maintain a multi-ethnic composition, with good relations between the Orthodox, Roman Catholic and Muslim communities in the city. I had the privilege of visiting Tuzla in late autumn 1995, to attend an international conference. On the Sunday of my visit, I worshipped in one of the Roman Catholic churches in the city. The service was packed, the people and the priest most welcoming. During the service an excellent choir sang an anthem: the choir consisted of Roman Catholic, Orthodox and Muslim men and women! After the service, some of us went to the old part of the city where five roads meet. There, on summer evenings, young people from Tuzla and its surrounding villages would gather to listen to music, to drink and chat together, to have fun in the way of young people throughout the world. A mortar bomb, fired from a neighbouring hillside, had landed precisely among their tables and had killed seventy of these young people outright. There can be little doubt that the bomb, targeted with accuracy and forethought, was the result of tribal hatred. Its devastating effects are remembered as vividly as the young people themselves.

Wherever you go in Bosnia, accounts of horrifying atrocities mar the surrounding beauty of the place. Nor is Ulster's situation so different. Trevor Williams, leader of the Corrymeela Community in Northern Ireland, writes of a conference he attended in Belfast entitled 'Boundaries and Bonds, Sectarianism, Identity and Reconciliation', addressed by the Croatian thinker Miroslav Volf:

> *The conference examined the boundaries and bonds so important for our identity and the necessity to cross those boundaries if we are to live in peace. Miroslav Volf is a Croatian and taught there during the war in former Yugoslavia. He told us how he had been asked*

by Professor Jürgen Moltmann, 'But can you embrace
a Cetnik?' He had just been arguing that Christians
ought to embrace our enemies as God has embraced us
in Christ. The notorious Serbian fighters, 'Cetniks', he
told me, had been herding people into concentration
camps, raping women, burning down churches and
destroying cities. Could he embrace a Cetnik, the ulti-
mate, evil 'other'? After a time, Miroslav replied: 'No,
I cannot, but, as a follower of Christ, I think I should
be able to . . .' In a vivid way Miroslav's task is the task
Northern Ireland faces.[1]

There are profound differences between Bosnia and Northern
Ireland, but the hard task of reconciliation is the same. The lug-
gage which has to be carried by unreconciled neighbours is the
fact of their imprisonment. Whether they see themselves as oppressed or as oppressors, victims or victors, both are in prison.
Beethoven's opera *Fidelio* tells the story of a prison and how
faithfulness can redeem the torment of such captivity. We hear
the prisoners' song, as they are allowed a brief respite from their
dark cells and clamber out into God's free air. There seems to be
a contrast between the conditions applying to prisoners and the
freedom enjoyed by prison officers and the other prison staff.
The truth is different. They are all prisoners of the system which
condemns those under sentence and those who guard them to a
common, shared imprisonment. The Church has a duty to question the effect prison has both on its victims and on those who,
superficially, appear to be their masters. The tragedy of Bosnia
and of Northern Ireland is that, in spite of the many heroic initiatives sustained by individuals and groups in both countries,
their leading politicians are imprisoned by the lack of God's reconciling grace. Yet hidden within that aspect of the torment of all
their peoples is this grain of hope. Once they recognize that they
are all equally imprisoned, both sides of the ethnic or tribal divide, the hope of a determination rising from the grassroots to
engage in reconciliation becomes significantly stronger. It is remarkable that the Good Friday Agreement of 1998 in Belfast was

strongly supported by paramilitaries from both extremes who had served a term in prison. Perhaps we should not be surprised.

Risking reconciliation

Let us roll back the centuries and go back to Ireland to find the secret that may lift the curse of Babel. St Patrick's Cathedral in Dublin has a 'Door of Reconciliation'. The story of the door reads as follows:

> *In 1492, two prominent Irish families, the Ormonds and Kildares, were in the midst of a bitter feud. Besieged by Gerald Fitzgerald, Earl of Kildare, Sir James Butler, Earl of Ormond, and his followers, took refuge in the chapter house of St Patrick's Cathedral, Dublin, bolting themselves in. As the siege wore on, the Earl of Kildare concluded that the feuding was foolish. Here were two families worshipping the same God, in the same church, living in the same country, trying to kill each other. So he called out to Sir James and, as an inscription in St Patrick's says today, 'undertook on his honour that he should receive no villanie'.*
>
> *Wary of 'some further treacherie', Ormond did not respond. So Kildare seized his spear, cut away a hole in the door and thrust his hand through. It was grasped by another hand inside the church, the door was opened and the two men embraced, thus ending the family feud.*²

The expression 'chancing one's arm' originated with Kildare's noble gesture. There is a lesson here for all of us who are engaged in 'family feuds', whether brother to brother, language to language, or nation to nation. If one of us would dare to 'chance his arm', perhaps that would be the first crucial step to the reconciliation we all unconsciously seek.

Chancing one's arm. There is risk in reconciliation. It takes a resolute person to risk that first gesture, take that first step, dare that cynical refusal. The Bible's stories can give us that resolution. The Father ran to meet the returning prodigal, ran to meet him before ever he had heard his son's carefully prepared speech. The risk is the real reconciling. Just as God risked the incarnation of his Son; just as God took the risk of creation – and takes it still, as he invites us at the threshold of a new millennium to try, yet again, to build the heaven of his kingdom on this earth.

Dialogue between faiths

This is a faithless world. So say most populist preachers. But is it? Often they say it at the climactic point of their sermons – at the very point when they go straight on to frighten their hearers out of faithlessness into faith. This suggests that, however boldly they proclaim this to be a faithless world, they do not really believe it. Perhaps it all depends how you measure the presence or absence of faith. Is faith really a matter of something measurable like church attendance? Surely it is something far deeper than that. I do not know whether the Britain of the 1990s is more faithless than the Britain of the 1890s or the 1790s. Nor am I sure what kind of thermometer would convince me that the spiritual temperature of today is higher or lower than that of yesterday. It may be that such an inquiry is beyond our computing. But if computers have been recruited to assist research into this matter, perhaps we should see what they have discovered.

The staff of the *World Christian Encyclopaedia* (Oxford, 1982) have devoted years of painstaking research to discovering statistical facts about the world's main religions. They estimated that at the time of their research, the 1980s, when there were 4.8 billion people living on this earth, 1.4 billion were nominally Christian, 7.23 million were Muslims, 5.83 million were Hindus and 2.74 million were Buddhists.[3] In brief, almost two thirds of the world's people are nominal adherents of the four largest faiths, to say nothing of the many smaller faith-systems and their followers. These statistics, however generalized, demonstrate that faith is a fact; and that dialogue between the faiths is a necessity. This necessity springs from our experience that the world has become a global neighbourhood, through ease of large-scale travel, instant world-wide communication and the close encounter of cultures. But it is not just proximity that should persuade Christians into inter-faith dialogue. In his speech at Mars Hill in Athens, Paul said that:

> *The God who made the world and everything in it, being Lord of heaven and earth, does not live in shrines made by man, nor is he served by human hands, as though he needed anything, since he himself gives to all men life and everything. And he made from one every nation of men to live on all the face of the earth, having determined allotted periods and the bounds of their habitation, that they should seek God, in the hope that they might feel after him and find him. Yet he is not far from each one of us, for 'in him we live and move and have our being'; as even some of your poets have said, 'for we are indeed his offspring'.*
> *(Acts 17.24–28).*

As the offspring of God, we are in direct sibling relationship with people of other faiths. It is as brothers and sisters in faith that we share in our common searching for God. Hans Küng speaks for the churches when he writes:

> *Ecumenical dialogue is today anything but the speciality of a few starry-eyed religious peaceniks. For the first time in history, it has now taken on the character of an urgent desideratum for world politics. It can help to make our earth more liveable, by making it more peaceful and more reconciled.*
>
> *There will be no peace among the peoples of this world without peace among the world religions.*
>
> *There will be no peace among the world religions without peace among the Christian churches.*
>
> *The community of the Church is an integral part of the world community.*
>
> *Ecumenism ad intra, concentrated on the Christian*

world, and ecumenism ad extra, *oriented toward the
whole inhabited earth, are interdependent.*
Peace is indivisible: it begins within us.[4]

I remember a coffee break during one of our 'sharing of faiths'
meetings in Glasgow's cosmopolitan West End, where my parish
was sited and the Sharing of Faiths Committee, which I chaired
for ten years, met. A Roman Catholic priest and I were chatting.
Our Sikh representative was a gifted maths teacher from the
Punjab, who had learned his remarkable accent from two years as
a bus conductor in Glasgow's East End. He told us he had a
question. He knew all about the continuing rivalry between
Celtic and Rangers on the football field – and on the buses. He
understood that this rivalry had religious roots. Could we ex-
pound to him the difference between Roman Catholic and Protestant Christianity? The priest and I looked at each other, looked
back at our Sikh friend – and then, in telepathic unison, said:
'No, we won't tell you the difference between us – it simply isn't
that important.' Were we wrong?

The philosopher Aristotle teaches that happiness is a by-
product. If you aim for it, you will miss it. On the other hand, if
you engage in a worthwhile pursuit with all your energy, you will
find happiness cheerfully clambering in the window of its own
accord. Does this teach us a lesson in our drive towards Christian
unity? Perhaps our faith-filled engagement in dialogue with people of other faiths will discover our Christian unity becoming
ever stronger – as a by-product of this engagement.

One of the disturbing features of many faiths is the recent
flourishing of fundamentalism. In particular, it affects Christianity, Judaism and Islam. This fundamentalism is more than a commitment to fundamentals, to the fundamental beliefs and values
of a tradition. It tends to be intolerant, authoritarian and unable
or unwilling to hear alternative views. While many Christians
would be sorry to see the Christian faith judged according to its
fundamentalist followers, that is very often what Christians do
when they judge Islam. There is an Islamophobia in Britain today
which refuses to take account of the undoubted fact that Islam

163

owns as wide a range of followers as the Christian faith. The Christians on our Sharing of Faiths Committee in Glasgow learned a great deal from the disciplined devotion of our Muslim members, from the patent piety of the Jews and from the self-deprecating cheerfulness of the Sikhs.

Inter-faith dialogue is not easy. It demands a faith commitment which has the confidence to listen to a different tune with courtesy, but without compromising the saving truth by which a Christian lives. In our dealings with people of other faiths, we have rarely behaved as Christians. No wonder they have a deeply distorted judgement of Christ, when his followers appear to show them a face that is not authentically his.

The need of the stranger

The hospitality we owe to the stranger who comes among us is well and widely understood. The Old Testament abounds with exhortations to care for the sojourner, the traveller, the person who, by definition, is not 'one of us'. Leviticus 19.34, Exodus 22.21, Deuteronomy 24.17 – these and many more passages urge us to meet the needs of the stranger. 'You shall love the stranger, for you were strangers in the land of Egypt.' The letter to the Hebrews takes up the same theme with its encouragement to welcome the stranger (Hebrews 13.1). We hardly require a second telling to respond to the stranger's need. What we are slow to recognize is our need of the stranger.

The stranger may have an identity, in nationality, colour or creed, that is different from the surrounding majority. For that reason, he or she has the potential for cracking our prejudices, breaking our horizons, disturbing our complacencies. That potential is precious. People of faith often have exclusive tendencies and none more so than the Jews. Yet the book of Ruth is not only one of the loveliest in the Bible, it is also a special favourite among Jews. It is read in its entirety at the Jewish celebration of Pentecost. Indeed, Ruth holds a position among Jews comparable, we are told, to that which Mary holds among Christians. It is not easy for us to know precisely what Ruth's contribution to her new nation was, but she demonstrates a steadfast loyalty at the personal level. 'Your people shall be my people and your God my God' (Ruth 1.16). These are some of the most strongly ecumenical words in the Bible. No Jew would question Ruth's contribution to Israel's history. Yet Ruth was an outsider; she was a Moabitess; she was one of 'them'. This suggests a truth which we may find uncomfortable. We need the stranger more than the stranger needs us.

John Calvin has always been one of my mentors. Unlike modern authors who try to produce a new title every year or two, Calvin wrote, over a period of twenty-three years, many new editions of one book, the *Institutes of the Christian Religion*. In this remarkable work, he lays a heavy emphasis on our knowledge of God. What seems to me certain is that our knowledge of God is diminished if we do not listen to the person who is seeking to know God from a different standpoint. Visitors to Edinburgh Castle may know the set of telescopes which, when properly focused, give the viewer a sight of the Forth Bridge, the architectural splendour of the New Town or maybe your aunt's living room in Granton. What could be more absurd than pulling a visitor away from his telescope and insisting that he looks through yours? It is the same with faith. 'Sir, we would see Jesus,' said the Greeks to Philip (John 12.21). If someone has gained knowledge of Jesus, we should listen to his testimony rather than insist that he can only know the Lord properly through our telescope. By listening to the other and sharing our insights with the other, her knowledge and ours will benefit – because each of us is limited by our own context. It is not sufficient, of course, to value the other's point of view for no other reason than that it is different. There must be a limit set to the degree of difference.

The World Council of Churches' Faith and Order Commission held an important conference at Santiago de Compostela in 1993. They examined the 'difficult issue of diversity', as they called it in their official report. Professor Jean-Marie Tillard writes in that report:

> *Unity is not a cluster of different elements, nor the sum*
> *total of them, nor a combination of them. It is rather*
> *what is expressed and revealed in them in all its rich*
> *variety. We are being challenged by this world where*
> *disintegration and division seem to be the work of dia-*
> *bolical powers, often latent in the guise of national and*
> *tribal loyalties, which they transform into masks of*
> *hate and war. That is why we have insisted on limits*
> *within which diversity is an enrichment and outside*
> *which it is not only unacceptable but also destructive.*
> *What is valid for humanity as such is obviously also*
> *valid for the Church. Certainly differences have their*
> *place in koinonia. They are the material out of which*
> *the Spirit creates reconciliation marked by mutual res-*
> *pect and complementarity. But not all differences are*
> *reconcilable. A change, a conversion must take place.*
> *The Faith and Order Commission, in its study on*
> *ecclesiology, will have to tackle this sensitive and diffi-*
> *cult issue. Is it not in fact the case that ecumenical*
> *responsibility and effectiveness have sometimes been*
> *somewhat blunted and obscured by decisions taken –*
> *and accepted by others, perhaps against their better*
> *judgement – out of a simple desire not to exclude?*
>
> *It is the undeniable vocation of Faith and Order to*
> *call the churches to visible unity rather than invite*
> *them generously to accept all diversities and all differ-*
> *ences. Faith and Order places diversity within unity*
> *and sees it in terms of unity. That is its specific contri-*
> *bution in the wide communion of workers in the ecu-*
> *menical movement. We stand on the threshold of a new*
> *way of living for humankind, and thus our service to*
> *the unification – not simply the unity – of Christians,*
> *rejecting clever compromises and exposing irreconcil-*
> *able differences, can help the churches to play their role*
> *as witnesses to the God and Father of our Lord Jesus*

> *Christ. For this God saves humanity by gathering us together, thereby rescuing us from the powers of sectarianism, of insensitive demands for more, and of imprisonment in our ego, which before our eyes are leading us to death. Differences can become the rich variety of koinonia only by passing through the crucible of a conversion in faith, hope and love. Otherwise they run the risk, for the slightest reason, of turning into hostility. This link made at this conference between koinonia and conversion is a fresh element.[5]*

The fact of this conversion, this *metanoia,* is the crux. We are not looking for the Church of yesterday, we are looking for a Church reborn, the Church of tomorrow. Yes, it will hopefully be recognizable by all our traditions, but it will not, it cannot, have four-square congruence with any of our current church traditions. That would be yesterday's Church.

Visible unity

There are those who take the view that the ecumenical movement at all levels, from the World Council to national and local Councils of Churches, has become obsessed with ecclesiastical joinery. The emphasis, they say, is on tinkering with structures rather than living the unity of the Spirit which is Christ's gift to his Church. Why devote energy, time and resources to a mechanistic approach, when the Church is a spiritual entity which cannot be captured by nuts and bolts? It sounds appealing and would let many church leaders off the hook. But the answer must be a resounding 'no' – certainly, a 'not yet'. The churches are committed to go for the goal of visible unity. It may not be full structural unity; it may not be the degree of sacramental unity which would satisfy all our churches; it may not even mean one church building and no more than one in every community. But the unity which is our goal has to be seen. It cannot hide behind the fudge of friendly fellowship or the vague screen of spiritual unity. These are both necessary, but they are intrinsically invisible. The requirement of visibility is not to catch headlines or win fame. The churches have to be reminded of the reason for their unity. It is to be visible to those who are not in the Church, to the world in fact – and for the world's sake. Unity is not to save church plant, or hard-gotten pounds and pence or even expensive paid personnel. It is not for the Church's sake at all. It is to be sought for the reason Jesus clearly stated: 'So that the world may believe.' Unity must be visible for the world's sake. The love which flows within the Trinity, between Father, Son and Holy Spirit in triangular communion, is the love which the Church is called, however falteringly, to enact. As the Church seeks to enact this quality of love, so the world may see it and learn how to live it. That remains the whole and holy purpose of our unity.

NOTES

1. Miroslav Volf, *Exclusion and Embrace* © Abingdon Press, Nashville, Tennessee, USA; used with permission.
2. 'Chancing one's arm' is from a postcard, the 'Door of Reconciliation' at St Patrick's Cathedral, Dublin; used with permission.
3. *World Christian Encyclopaedia* (Oxford University Press, 1982), pp.777ff.
4. Hans Küng, *Christianity and the World Religions* (Collins, London, 1985), p.443.
5. Jean-Marie Tillard, *On the Way to a Fuller Koinonia*, Official Report of the 5th World Council of Churches' Faith and Order Conference (Geneva, 1993).

Eight

FOR GOD'S SAKE . . . UNITY
Elizabeth Templeton

> *The Kingdom*
> *It's a long way off but inside it*
> *There are quite different things going on:*
> *Festivals at which the poor man*
> *Is king and the consumptive is*
> *Healed; mirrors in which the blind look*
> *At themselves and love looks at them*
> *Back; and industry is for mending*
> *The bent bones and the minds fractured*
> *By life. It's a long way off, but to get*
> *There takes no time and admission*
> *Is free, if you will purge yourself*
> *Of desire, and present yourself with*
> *Your need only and the simple offering*
> *Of your faith, green as a leaf.*
> R. S. Thomas, Collected Poems 1945–1990

Now God and Satan were walking in the cool of the day in the garden of time. And Satan said to God: 'Do you not regret this garden you have planted for the end of time? It is beautiful and comely, with its fruits and its foliage and its rivers, but it can never be tasted by the sons and daughters of men.'

'You have too little faith and hope and love, my dear Satan,' replied God. 'This garden is prepared for the Jews and for the nations, and for the whole cosmos, for their nourishment and their joy. And it is planted and fertilized and tended by the creativity of my Spirit and the costly energy of my Son, and by my patience. How then can it fail to delight the daughters and sons of men?'

'Because you have been foolish enough to give them freedom and history. You could have made them like the angels, seeing your glory, at no distance from your beauty, eternally bound to you in wonder and praise.'

'Ah, Satan,' said God sadly, 'I rather fear that is *your* way of holding sway, by your insistent presence with those to whom you offer delight. My way is different. When I walked in that first garden, it is true that I longed for communion with this fragile earth I had made. I longed to see all of it in harmony; but I am not a manager, I am a lover. And lovers do not constrain love by displays of grandeur, by *force majeure*, not even by their constant brilliant presence. They drop hints; they offer gifts; they issue invitations. But the freedom of the other, even her freedom not to love back, is paramount. Sorcerers offer love potions. Lovers do not use them.'

Satan was nettled. 'You are insulting my integrity,' he retorted. 'I too love creation and want it to taste glory: not to be fragmented and diseased and crippled. I too want the mountains to leap for joy and the trees of the field to clap their hands. I simply think you have gone the wrong way about it. Good parenting often means telling children they have to be in a certain place at a certain time; making them eat the food that is good for them; insisting that they sleep; removing options that will harm them. How could you leave them to it, this ridiculous, puny Adam-Eve, to name creation for you, attend to what you said, have access to the tree of knowledge?'

'I rather thought,' said God drily, 'that had something to do with you!'

'Not the access! If you knew they would be temptable, if you knew they would want the knowledge of good and evil, more than life itself, why did you not fence the tree off until they had wisdom to understand? If they had tasted the tree of life first, the knowledge could have followed. They would have known the joy of life. They could have grown into understanding. My objection was the lie! The knowledge of good and evil doesn't make you die!'

'Oh, Satan, Satan – I have never grudged them life. I *gave* them life through all the slow, patient, risky evolution of the earth. But I knew that they could not share *my* life unless their knowledge flowed out of free relationship to me. You cannot be deathless unless your knowledge is love-knowledge! You cannot be one with God if you seek to be God without God. You invited them to believe they would be like gods. *That* was the lie. I wanted them, right from the beginning, to share the communion and freedom of my being, for their sakes and for my sake. I made history and time and culture in which to plant the seed of that longing. But you wanted to do a rush job: instant pre-packed godhood. I wanted them to grow into desire, attraction, response, delight, a sense of their identity with the love between us, Father, Son, Spirit; a knowledge that they were not swamped, overwhelmed, submerged, absorbed; confidence that they were particular, irreplaceable, distinct. I wanted them to know they belonged to their new and precious earth, made out of nothing, in sheer love and freedom, not because they were screwed down to it by divine jealousy. And that the whole earth was welcome to share my life, unforced, undazzled, adding to me.'

'Isn't that, if you don't mind my saying so, a bit of an ego-trip?' asked Satan. 'To put humanity through all the pains and woes of history so that you might be added to? In any case how can God be *added* to? I thought it was a defining characteristic of God to be all in all, self-sufficient, beyond need. If you *needed* to create, you are an ungodlike God: you can't add anything to infinity! But even if your ambitions were genuinely for the sake of the earth and not for your own sake, it didn't work. The earth is a mess – fragmented, abused, neglected by the sons and daughters of Adam. This "unity" you envisaged, of a cosmos in communion with you, has not come off.'

'We are still working at it,' said God, 'and will work at it till the end of time. And in the end, because the deepest belonging of the earth is in our oneness, I trust them to come home.'

How does one write about what is true 'for God's sake'? The pen boggles! We know what it means to think about human need, longing, fulfilment and so on. But God – classically described as 'without parts or passions' – how do we talk of God's needs, longings, fulfilment? Is God not already full, needing nothing? How can anything *matter* to God? Are we not simply projecting human-zone images, psychological models of the self, on to this God who is not an 'ego', not a 'personality' in our modern sense? Is it not hubris beyond belief to speculate on what is 'for God's sake'?

The Bible, of course, does it boldly. God is angry, grieved, offers choices, remembers, forgets, decides – and so on. He is a larger-than-life 'character' in many of the biblical narratives – full of power, able to smite people dead, to produce bigger and better miracles than the enemy, to start and stop the rain.

The major theological problem for twenty-first-century Christians is that this God no longer convinces, at least in the culture of post-modern Europe and the westernized world. If you are sick, you go and see a doctor and ask about symptoms, sources of infection, prognosis, treatment etc., although you may also pray about it. If there are droughts or floods, the world attends meteorological conferences about global warming and climate change. We do not, on the whole, expect God to overrule the patterns of weather, which human behaviour has helped to modify and natural forces generate.

The cosmic watcher-and-minder in the sky has, for most of the population, even for many in the Christian population, become implausible – Blake's 'Nobodaddy'. No God who had the power to intervene, and did not intervene at Auschwitz, can be hymned for rescuing his people. Whatever God's love means, it does not mean that the brokenness and pain of creation is going to be short-circuited. Imagination is very nearly defeated by how to maintain the affirmation that love is at the heart of things in so distressed a world.

Very nearly, but not quite.

In spite of all the awareness that the twentieth century has given us of psychological defence-mechanisms, projection, social constructions of reality, corporate myth, stories fabricated to legitimize power, for me the hope of God's reality remains.

It may or may not be failure to say it is 'hope' rather than 'knowledge'. But it is the hope on which I risk my life, which sets the direction of my being and frames my view of everything else I encounter. That, of course, is an overstatement which verges on pomposity! At ten to eight on weekday mornings, as the scramble to find the gym kit, the homework diary, the missing bus pass, reaches its climax, I have no thought of God!

Nevertheless, on the far side of seven years of real agnosticism, loss of belief and loss of the ability to worship with conviction, I have so far lived the rest of my adulthood with the hope that God is around us, ahead of us and among us, not a projection of human imagination and desire, but an inviting reality.

With that hope of God, the exploration of ecumenism has gone hand in hand. To say why unity is 'for God's sake' can only be, for me, a rehearsal of my story of encounter and enlargement in relation to this God.

I had a lucky start. My father was a Christian pacifist who, precisely because he believed that the gospel abolished the category of 'enemy', refused to fight in the Second World War and went to prison for it. My Presbyterian minister, throughout my whole growth to adulthood, was years ahead of the trend, sharing key points of the Christian year with other denominations and steadily nourishing his congregation with the riches of catholic Christendom.

At the same time, I absorbed through other pores the atmosphere of West of Scotland Catholic/Protestant suspicion. I remember my father taking me, at about the age of eight, into Clyde Street in Glasgow – his birthday, ironically, being on 12 July, the day of the big Orange Lodge Parade. He stood as the pipes and drums passed and said, 'Look at the hate on these faces; never let religion make you like that.' But along the road from our house, when the snow fell, the local Protestant school and the local Catholic school would hurl snowballs across the road to shouts of 'Dirty Catholics' and 'Dirty Protestants'. My adult memory harbours a conversation (why?) in which my mother, talking to a neighbour about a new Italian arrival in the street, said, 'She's a Catholic, but she's very nice.' The 'but' hovered for many years.

Soon after I went to secondary school my Protestant fervour increased. A close encounter with the Scripture Union resulted in my salvation, with the corollary that the rest of the world, including my parents, my wee brother, my minister, my church, and certainly Roman Catholics, were damned. This almost erotic intensity lasted for two years, until a camp commandant interrogated our righteousness (can child abuse be extended to cover such things?) and asked me if I had suffered persecution as a result of my conversion. 'Oh yes,' I said, 'they think I'm funny for refusing to do French homework on Sundays. And they don't believe you have to ask the Lord Jesus into your life to be saved.'

'Well done,' Commy X said. 'You know that Jesus said, "I come not with peace, but with a sword."'

Scales fell from my eyes, and I hope I lost a measure of adolescent priggishness. My father's costly love of peace was better than this cheap self-righteousness. My bones knew it, and although I remained, for friendship's sake, a member of my school SU, I never believed it again.

Meanwhile my gentle, generous minister, ignoring my accusations that his church was rather worse than Laodicea, continued to feed me: *The Cloud of Unknowing*, St John of the Cross, Francis de Sales, Evelyn Underhill, Von Hügel. The eroticism transferred! By the time I arrived at New College to start my BD, I had vast amounts of Catholic spirituality under my belt and in my bloodstream, and had assumed, wrongly, that this was the normal diet of devout Presbyterian teenagers. It was a terrible shock to find some of my fellow students debating whether Catholics were Christians!

What had brought me to New College was the desire to know

how anybody thought faith was credible. Four years in the Arts Faculty of Glasgow University had challenged me to the limits of my faith. Men of huge integrity – among them Keith Ward, who was in those days an empiricist of the A. J. Ayer variety; and Robin Downie, who once said to me: 'Elizabeth, to believe this stuff you either have to be a fool or a knave: and you're not a fool' – pressed me to face whether there were any reasonable grounds for belief, and I could no longer find them.

There was, of course, the option of celebrating the foolishness of belief, the Tertullian paradox of believing *because* it was absurd, but that seemed a cop-out if this God really was to be loved with heart and *mind* and soul and strength. If I had to disintegrate, abandon my mind, not even find unity in my own existence, what was the point in pursuing a God who was allegedly interested in the unity of all things?

So a kind of darkness set in. My spiritual comfort, out of my ecumenical reading, was that this was standard, that people came through it, that it was a stage in a process of deepening, that it did not mean the abandonment of God. But the lived, day-to-day *feel* was that there was no God, that faith was a fiction, that the creed bounced off the wall, that the Church was on a wild goose chase, that it was much easier to explain why people needed to have faith than to justify the faith they had.

What released me from *that* imprisonment (clearly I have some gift for jumping into prisons) was getting to know John Zizioulas, who came to teach at New College soon after I began lecturing there as a kind of 'licensed agnostic'. (When I went to discuss my application for the job with the man who was to be my professor, I confessed through well-brushed teeth that I could not take my money for telling students what the truth was. 'Don't worry, Elizabeth,' he said, 'there are plenty of us who can do that.')

John is now Metropolitan of Pergamum, the theological adviser to the Ecumenical Patriarchate in Istanbul. But when I first met him he was a lay theologian and proud of it. He was the one whom I overheard saying, 'Of course, the best theologians in the

West in the 20th century are the existentialist atheists.' He was the one who introduced me to Sartre's famous scenario where a man waits in a crowded café for his friend, and the friend does not come. And Sartre writes, 'My friend who was not there was more present than all the people around me in the place.'

That rang true. This God who was not around was more present than the busy world.

Gradually, as I came to know John – though I never knew him better than through that first remembered remark – a completely new world crossed my ecumenical vision, that of Eastern Orthodoxy.

The presence of the Orthodox Church is still minimal in the UK, although it is the only denomination growing, apart from the right-wing Protestant evangelical cults and sects. That is a matter for regret, because to my mind the altercations between Western Protestant and Western Catholic theologies are like pimples in comparison with those of the Christian East (Russian and Greek Orthodoxy being the two main named inheritors) and the Christian West (everything from Augustine onwards).

In the West, we basically take the Aristotelian line, articulated fully by Aquinas and taken to its horrendous logical conclusion by Calvin, that God is First Cause, that he determines, for example, whether or not a mother shall have enough milk to feed her child.

Eastern Orthodoxy places causality differently, as a manifestation of the Fall from which God seeks to free us. Miracle is not super-causality; it is the release *from* causality into the freedom of God which lets God be human and humanity become God. It is not the axiom of Aristotle's logic and biology, 'A = A', but the astonishing openness of God who says: 'I will be who I will be.' I, A, will become B. You, B, will become A. These constrictions of 'nature' are not of my making. 'Love's function is to fabricate unknownness.'

For me, the exhilaration of this vision is what nerves the risk-taking which our timid churches are so bad at. Of course, as human beings, we like to have things taped, to know where we

176

are, to divide into insiders and outsiders, to define the goodies and the baddies. And indeed, at its empirical worst, the Orthodox Church is as bad as any other at that game.

But deep within the spirituality and liturgy of Orthodoxy is the gut sense of human solidarity which grows out of God's solidarity in Christ with the whole human condition. So, for example, in Dostoevsky's novels, the saint and the sinner each recognize the other as themselves – are in the same person, like Alyosha's dying nurse who, after a visibly blameless life, utters the words, 'I am responsible for everything.'

It is not surprising that the core of Orthodox worship has to do with the unbreakable circularity of the Trinity, reduced so often in Western iconography to 'two men and a bird', with the Holy Spirit as a kind of post-Christ messenger who can reach the parts inaccessible to Father and Son.

The point of the Rublev ikon and its counterparts is, however, that every member of the company of the Trinity, points, by eye or hand, away from himself to the other, and all end up with their energies focused on the Eucharist, the event *par excellence* where A becomes not-A; where heaven and earth fuse; where the Church is at home in the kingdom; where I am so identified with whatever neighbour that there is no one on earth to whom I dare say, 'I can do without you.'

Yet humanly I contentedly do without lots of people; and some of those I do deal with I would love, at a psychological level, to be shot of!

It has never seemed to me a problem to span denominations. University nurture in chaplaincy centre and SCM made it clear that most of these barricades were irrelevant to life and death, and I know people in almost every branch of the Church who are kinsfolk.

The difficult task is to span the yawning gulf between those in all the denominations who believe that God is disclosed in absolute, necessary structures, creeds, orders of ministry, voting procedures, etc., and, on the other hand, those who believe that God is disclosed in the provisionality and risk, the trial and error of all statements, dogmas, structures and forms, in the constant discovery that we are not who we thought we were.

Facing that discovery with exhilaration and good hope rather than with panic and dismay seems to me the Church's vocation. Nothing else echoes the delight and patience God takes in his wandering creation, exploring space and time for the millions of years of life on earth.

That is no way to deny the 'passion' aspects of our co-existence. Only those with shut eyes can be happy-clappy in a world so broken. But the Christian vision of God's unity with us involves the solidarity of God himself, in the person of Jesus, with all the depths of the human condition, the very harrowing of hell. God's presence with us is not some euphoric 'dwam' of sweetness and light; it is the commitment to take the world's pain into the very life of God. Technically, the ancient theologies said, the Father cannot suffer. And all talk about the inner relationships of the Trinity seem to me beyond articulation. But I believe the intuition of William Blake's sketch for a drawing of the Trinity, where the Father cradles the cruciform Son in a *pietà* position, bowed over him in the intimacy of a grieving lover, and the Spirit canopies both, under outstretched hovering wings.

This sense of Trinity as the way God is, while formally acknowledged in all my childhood nurture, actually comes more alive in Orthodox worship and spirituality than in any other. And it has, for me, become the most precious image of that freedom-in-communion and communion-in-freedom which is, I believe, the horizon of our living.

Nevertheless, I am alarmed by the fact that belief in the Trinity has become the *sine qua non* of acceptance within the formal structures of the ecumenical movement, determining, for instance, the fate of new applications for membership of the World Council of Churches and of the Council of Churches for Britain and Ireland. There are many reasons why the simpler and earlier acclamation, 'Jesus is Lord', was more inclusive, not least in relation to Unitarians, who have a proper cause of grievance at the admission of the Religious Society of Friends while they, with their parallel heritage of non-conformist openness, are excluded.

Over the last thirty years, I have been involved at various levels of ecumenical life, with the former BCC and the new British and Irish ecumenical instruments, with the Multilateral Conversations, with the World Alliance of Reformed Churches, the Conference of European Churches and the World Council of Churches. I have also worked locally with an ecumenical project called Threshold, which works post-denominationally to support theological exploration for all comers, and have been involved with CCBI's creative Ecumenical Spirituality Project.

In my spectrum of friends, even of Christian friends, there are polar opposites.

Some of those I love and admire have spent decades in slow and patient negotiations, discussions, consultations, attending endless meetings, processing endless documents, nudging assemblies, synods, presbyteries, to inch millimetres forward in ecumenical co-existence.

Others have left all that behind, with emotions ranging from despair to scornful anger. They do not believe that denominational reintegration, should that ever be possible, will do anything significant for God, or even for the life of the Church. They believe that the causes of separation, mostly to do with doctrinal squabbling and political power struggles, are not areas of creativity, and should be abandoned in favour of living church manifestations of celebration, service and solidarity which make clear the unity of creation, not conditional on creed, class, race, gender and denominational history.

I must confess that I am caught in a huge ambivalence about all this, which makes my speculations as to what God makes of it all rather cloudy!

The proper balance between patience and impatience eludes me.

There is a nice, wicked and true ecumenical story from Geneva about an Anglican bishop who was escorting a visiting Orthodox patriarch along WCC corridors. Rather mischievously he asked him what he thought of the Churches Ecumenical Decade in

Solidarity with Women. 'Decade! Decade!' replied the distinguished visitor. 'What has God to do with decades?'

Given the recent Black Sea voyage of Orthodox heavyweights, in which the pollution of creation was named as heresy, things may be changing; but the desperate slowness of ecumenical advance at the formal level is something I find hard to live with creatively. Does God really care about the *'Filioque'*? About bishops or their absence in the structures of church life? About the ordination of women? About the reports of Doctrine Commissions?

My suspicion is, increasingly, that such preoccupations are not actually for God's sake, but for *our* sakes; that we are such prisoners of our history, language and culture that we make theological mountains out of what must seem molehills to God.

That is not at all to say that theology is not worth doing. The category of 'truth' is a vital one, and the Faith and Order agendas of the ecumenical movement take that seriously. But I think that the notion that we can verbally articulate the truth of God needs correction from the deep apophatic traditions of the Church, as well as from our own century's painful awareness of the way words slip and slide. The painful and patient attempts to hammer out documents like 'Baptism, Eucharist and Ministry' or 'Confessing the Apostolic Faith' are certainly motivated, on the whole, by the *desire* for unity. But I find it increasingly hard to believe that structural unity should be conditional on theological consensus.

What it should depend on, and arise from, is the desire in us which, we believe, echoes the desire in God that all things return to enjoy the glory of being, no longer threatened by death and disintegration.

Now, of course, not all Christians do believe that. Many actually live a theology of vindictiveness, where their own hope of salvation (like my evangelical teenage one) depends on the satisfactory damnation of someone else: the heretic, the blasphemer, the promiscuous, the rich, the infidel.

This is quite unlike the spirit of, say, the Desert Fathers, where the holy man would offer himself to hell in order to save some-one else, or of Countess Kathleen in Yeats's play.

Within the scriptures, there are both exclusivist and inclusivist theologies, both in the Old Testament and the New. How we re-late to these will be a complex matter, including nurture, dis-position, historical awareness and faith conviction.

All I can say is that a God who is, in the end, beaten by our sin is no God. And in so far as we say with integrity, 'I believe in the Holy Ghost ... the forgiveness of sins ... the resurrection of the dead', we *need* the courage to anticipate God's inclusiveness in our ecclesial life.

I agree wholeheartedly with Maxwell Craig that 'spiritual unity' is not enough, and is indeed usually the cop-out of those who are really quite content with the *status quo*.

I agree too that ecumenical matrimony, like secular matri-mony, cannot be a matter of mere sentimental attachment. Liv-ing and loving involves us in questions of death: whose life threatens ours? Whose life do we threaten? How do conflicts get resolved when they appear to be bound up with people's very identity, as in Palestine, Belfast or Nigeria?

Where to find the psychological and political strength to be willing to lay down one's life for one's friends, let alone one's enemies, is a hard question, even more for institutions than for individuals. But I am clear that the Church does *not* act for God's sake unless that is its earthed witness. Yet all our churches tend to live with the concern for self-preservation in the gut, if not on the tongue, of their expressed desires. (As one of the ACTS Re-view consultants put it: The churches have all put their cards on the table. Unfortunately, they all have another pack behind their backs!)

What would 'unity for God's sake' be like?

It would be a willingness to welcome without limits, to take delight in the otherness of the other, to renounce all desire to control, to share in mutuality and trust all the resources at one's disposal. It would involve pooling capital, both financial and in terms of personnel, and making no unilateral decisions out of earshot of other churches, or without their endorsement.

It would involve our contrition and repentance at how, through the history of Christendom, we have confused 'kingdom of God' with 'empire', forgetting that our particular 'king' was a foot-washer, a mixer with 'undesirables', a subversive, whose way of fulfilling the law so threatened its custodians that they could not abide him.

It would, I think, at best involve our inability or refusal to eat at the eucharistic table without one another's sharing being achieved. Jesus said that he would not drink the fruit of the vine until he drank it new in his father's kingdom. The Church assumes that in the Eucharist that kingdom is tasted, anticipated by those who partake. But we seem to have lost the sense that this *cannot* be the kingdom if we cannot share even with our fellow Christians, let alone with people of other faiths, and with the nations.

Unity for God's sake means unity which is discontented with the status of 'outsiderness' for any human being or community, and certainly with outsiderness which is imposed by those of us who are insiders, in the face of the explicit desire of others to belong, to follow, to share.

There was a moving story told at Santiago de Compostela during the most recent Faith and Order Conference. One of the bishops of the Church of South India described how a Hindu friend came frequently to his church. On one occasion he came forward at the Eucharist. The bishop, somewhat startled, gave him the elements and later sought him out to explain what communion meant. A few weeks later, the man came back and again presented himself at the altar. With rather more misgivings, the bishop again gave him bread and wine, but afterwards said, with some indignation, 'Did you not understand what I said? To share this meal you have to make a commitment to the Lord Jesus Christ. You are a Hindu. You have not made that commitment.' To which the Hindu replied, 'When I read your Scriptures, I find that the Jews did not have to stop being Jews to love and follow

Jesus. Why do I have to stop being a Hindu?' The force of that question was, for the bishop, revelatory.

Clearly, there is more similarity in many ways between Judaism, Christianity and Islam in terms of scriptural heritage and religious style, than between the three of them and the faiths of Far-Eastern origin. But it is precisely because, in Christian tradition, there *can* only be one God, that we have to give some account of that God's relation to the whole inhabited earth – the Buddhists, the Sikhs, the Pagans, the Baha'i, the agnostics, the humanists, the unlabelled people who live a day at a time with whatever crops up: birth, death, family conflict, good times, bad times.

The scenario as portrayed for much of Christian history has been that God's relationship to all these communities is one only of judgement, and of a call to repentance; never of support and endorsement.

I no longer believe that.

My work with the Christian Education Movement (which in spite of its name – or rather, because of it – is committed to multi-faith education), my contact with people of other faiths, and my reading of other Christians (Thomas Merton/Kenneth Cracknell/Raimondo Panikkar, who have spent lifetimes in deepening dialogue across faith boundaries) are increasingly convincing me that ecumenism will be trivial unless it engages pretty fast in inter-faith dialogue.

It will also be trivial if it does not seek to engage with the complex world of twenty-first-century Europe, and how we relate to the rest of the world.

On the surface, we are the 'developed world'. But over and over again we are manifestly *underdeveloped*: we have lost touch with the earth – hence secular protests about road-building and nuclear waste disposal. We have lost touch with our shared humanity – hence secular protests about racism, the rights of gay and lesbian people to fulfilling love, handicapped access to fullness of life, women and 'glass ceilings', stillness and wisdom.

These are not only issues in which the churches could and

should lead if we really believed in the inclusive God who nourishes our hopes of unity. They are issues in which, historically, the Church has dragged its feet long after the secular world, or large sections of it, has expressed and manifested real commitment, real discovery.

This concrete, political history means, I think, that we should renounce all claims to prophecy for the time being: for God's sake! For God, I suspect, is more adventurous, more risk-taking, more generous, more open than any church we inhabit. And *all* our churches are afraid of God.

It seems to me that many of the groups which are *not* afraid, which are already tasting the joy of post-denominational and even post-Christian living, cannot see a way of being positively involved in the structural life of the official ecumenical movement. Meanwhile, many properly quota-agreed meetings at Dunblane, or 121 George Street, or the Catholic Bishops' Conference, or the Synod Offices are not actually enabling the new life which many Christians know in their bones is the only future. Indeed, some militate against it; for they constantly refer back to the denominational past and are represented by people for whom that identity is primary (often heavily clerical and predominantly male?!).

Denominations are not, I believe, genuinely human structures. Like 'nationhood', a denomination is a construct. It serves some functions, but it denies or ignores many more: whether people are authoritarian or permissive; whether they love art or have no feel for it; whether they trust or distrust structures; whether they have been more wounded or more healed by their contact with Christianity; whether they love theology or fear it; whether their children feel at home in the family's religious culture or estranged by it; whether they bring their bodies to worship or leave them behind; whether they enjoy the secular world or hate and fear it. These are the deeper ecumenical questions.

How dare anyone say what God enjoys, hopes for, invests

energy in?!

All I can say is that if God 'cares more' about confessional consensus than about the possibility that all children eat enough and laugh, I do not want that unity.

If God 'cares more' about the proper rites of baptism and ordination than about our ability to love one another across boundaries of faith/unfaith/class/religion/colour/sex/education/status, this is not a God I want to worship, nor one I believe in.

As human beings, we live in a cosmos faced with death.

Unity, 'for God's sake', is about the strange hope that there is life stronger than death – that 'quite different things are going on'.

That is unprovable. But maybe worth believing.

THE IONA COMMUNITY

The Iona Community is an ecumenical Christian community, founded in 1938 by the late Lord MacLeod of Fuinary (the Revd George MacLeod DD) and committed to seeking new ways of living the Gospel in to-day's world. Gathered around the rebuilding of the ancient monastic buildings of Iona Abbey, but with its original inspiration in the poorest areas of Glasgow during the Depression, the Community has sought ever since the 'rebuilding of the common life', bringing together work and worship, prayer and politics, the sacred and the secular in ways that reflect its strongly incarnational theology.

The Community today is a movement of some 200 Members, over 1,400 Associate Members and about 1,600 Friends. The Members — women and men from many backgrounds and denominations, most in Britain, but some overseas — are committed to a rule of daily prayer and Bible reading, sharing and accounting for their use of time and money, regular meeting and action for justice and peace.

The Iona Community maintains three centres on Iona and Mull: Iona Abbey and the MacLeod Centre on Iona, and Camas Adventure Camp on the Ross of Mull. Its base is in Community House, Glasgow, where it also supports work with young people, the Wild Goose Resource and Worship Groups, a bimonthly magazine (*Coracle*) and a publishing house (Wild Goose Publications).

For further information on the Iona Community please contact:
The Iona Community
Pearce Institute,
840 Govan Road
Glasgow G51 3UU
T. 0141 445 4561; F. 0141 445 4295
e-mail: ionacomm@gla.iona.org.uk

OTHER TITLES FROM
WILD GOOSE PUBLICATIONS

SONGBOOKS with full music
(titles marked * have companion cassettes)
SEVEN SONGS OF MARY*, John Bell
SEVEN PSALMS OF DAVID*, John Bell
SEVEN PSALMS OF DAVID - PACK OF OCTAVOS* John Bell
LOVE AND ANGER*, John Bell and Graham Maule
WHEN GRIEF IS RAW, John Bell and Graham Maule
THE LAST JOURNEY - PACK OF 15 OCTAVOS* John Bell
THE LAST JOURNEY reflections*, John Bell
THE COURAGE TO SAY NO: 23 SONGS FOR EASTER & LENT*
J Bell & G Maule
GOD NEVER SLEEPS – PACK OF 12 OCTAVOS* John Bell
COME ALL YOU PEOPLE, Shorter Songs for Worship* John Bell
PSALMS OF PATIENCE, PROTEST AND PRAISE* John Bell
HEAVEN SHALL NOT WAIT (Wild Goose Songs Vol.1)* J Bell & Graham
Maule
ENEMY OF APATHY (Wild Goose Songs Vol.2) J Bell & Graham Maule
LOVE FROM BELOW (Wild Goose Songs Vol.3)* John Bell & Graham
Maule
INNKEEPERS & LIGHT SLEEPERS* (for Christmas) John Bell
MANY & GREAT (Songs of the World Church Vol.1)* John Bell (ed./arr.)
SENT BY THE LORD (Songs of the World Church Vol.2)* John Bell
(ed./arr.)
FREEDOM IS COMING* Anders Nyberg (ed.)
PRAISING A MYSTERY, Brian Wren
BRING MANY NAMES, Brian Wren

CASSETTES & CDs (titles marked † have companion songbooks)
Cassette, SEVEN SONGS OF MARY/SEVEN PSALMS OF DAVID, †
John Bell (guest conductor)
CD, SEVEN SONGS OF MARY/SEVEN PSALMS OF DAVID, †
John Bell (guest conductor)
Cassette, LOVE AND ANGER, † Wild Goose Worship Group
CD, THE LAST JOURNEY, † John Bell (guest conductor)
Cassette, THE LAST JOURNEY, † John Bell (guest conductor)
Cassette, IONA ABBEY, WORSHIP FROM EASTER WEEK (ed/arr
 Steve Butler)

Cassette, THE COURAGE TO SAY NO † Wild Goose Worship Group
Cassette, GOD NEVER SLEEPS † John Bell (guest conductor)
CD, GOD NEVER SLEEPS † John Bell (guest conductor)
Cassette, COME ALL YOU PEOPLE † Wild Goose Worship Group
CD, PSALMS OF PATIENCE, PROTEST AND PRAISE † Wild Goose
Worship Group
Cassette, PSALMS OF PATIENCE, PROTEST AND PRAISE † WGWG
Cassette, HEAVEN SHALL NOT WAIT † Wild Goose Worship Group
Cassette, LOVE FROM BELOW † Wild Goose Worship Group
Cassette, INNKEEPERS & LIGHT SLEEPERS † (for Christmas) WGWG
Cassette, MANY AND GREAT † Wild Goose Worship Group
Cassette, SENT BY THE LORD † Wild Goose Worship Group
Cassette, FREEDOM IS COMING † Fjedur
Cassette, TOUCHING PLACE, A, Wild Goose Worship Group
Cassette, CLOTH FOR THE CRADLE, Wild Goose Worship Group
Cassette, SIGNS OF FIRE, Ian Fraser

DRAMA BOOKS

EH JESUS...YES PETER No. 1, John Bell and Graham Maule
EH JESUS...YES PETER No. 2, John Bell and Graham Maule
EH JESUS...YES PETER No. 3, John Bell and Graham Maule

PRAYER/WORSHIP BOOKS

MEDITATIONS FROM THE IONA COMMUNITY, Ian Reid
CLOTH FOR THE CRADLE, Worship Resources and Readings for
Advent, Christmas and Epiphany, Wild Goose Worship Group
THE PILGRIMS' MANUAL, Christopher Irvine
THE PATTERN OF OUR DAYS, Kathy Galloway (ed.)
PRAYERS AND IDEAS FOR HEALING SERVICES, Ian Cowie
HE WAS IN THE WORLD: Meditations for Public Worship,
John Bell
EACH DAY AND EACH NIGHT: Prayers from Iona in the Celtic
Tradition, Philip Newell
IONA COMMUNITY WORSHIP BOOK,
THE WHOLE EARTH SHALL CRY GLORY, George MacLeod
STRANGE FIRE, Ian Fraser

OTHER BOOKS

CHASING THE WILD GOOSE: The Story of the Iona Community,
Ron Ferguson

DREAMING OF EDEN: Reflections on Christianity and Sexuality, Kathy Galloway (ed.)

THE PROSPECT OF HEAVEN: Musings of an Enquiring Believer, Frederick Levison

THE OWL AND THE STEREO, David Osborne

COLUMBA: Pilgrim and Penitent, Ian Bradley

THE EARTH UNDER THREAT: A Christian Perspective, Ghillean Prance

THE MYTH OF PROGRESS, Yvonne Burgess

WHAT IS THE IONA COMMUNITY?

PUSHING THE BOAT OUT: New Poetry, Kathy Galloway (ed.)

EXILE IN ISRAEL: A Personal Journey with the Palestinians, Runa Mackay

FALLEN TO MEDIOCRITY: CALLED TO EXCELLENCE, Erik Cramb

REINVENTING THEOLOGY AS THE PEOPLE'S WORK, Ian Fraser

STARTING WHERE WE ARE, Kathy Galloway

STATES OF BLISS & YEARNING, John L. Bell